DANISH YEARBOOK
OF
PHILOSOPHY

VOLUME 41

DANISH YEARBOOK OF PHILOSOPHY

VOLUME 41
2006

MUSEUM TUSCULANUM PRESS
UNIVERSITY OF COPENHAGEN 2007

Published for
Dansk Filosofisk Selskab
in cooperation with
the Philosophical Societies of Aarhus and Odense
and with financial support from
the Danish Research Council for the Humanities

*

EDITORIAL BOARD:

FINN COLLIN
University of Copenhagen
Chairman

JØRGEN HUGGLER
Danish University of Education

UFFE JUUL JENSEN
University of Aarhus

STIG ANDUR PEDERSEN
Roskilde University Centre

ERICH KLAWONN
Odense University

HANS SIGGAARD JENSEN
Copenhagen Business School

MOGENS PAHUUS
Aalborg University

LARS GUNDERSEN
University of Aarhus

*

Articles for consideration and all editorial communications should be sent in three copies to:
Danish Yearbook of Philosophy
University of Copenhagen, Department of Philosophy
Njalsgade 80, DK 2300 Copenhagen S, Denmark

Business communications, including subscriptions and orders for reprints, should
be addressed to the publishers:
MUSEUM TUSCULANUM PRESS
Njalsgade 126
DK 2300 Copenhagen S
Denmark

*

© 2007 DANISH YEARBOOK OF PHILOSOPHY
COPENHAGEN, DENMARK
PRINTED IN DENMARK
BY SPECIAL-TRYKKERIET VIBORG A-S

ISBN 978 87 635 0699 1
ISSN 0070-2749

CONTENTS

Alfred Nordmann: *Collapse of Distance:*
    Epistemic Strategies of Science and Technoscience 7

Mirko Wischke: *Vom Jenseits des Bekannten.*
    Adorno über Darstellung, Sprache und Rhetorik 35

Morten Ebbe Juul Nielsen: *Cultural Rights and*
    Liberal Multiculturalism 51

Jan Faye: *Quantum Realism: The Interpretation of an Interpretation?* 83

Peter Øhrstrøm: *Towards an Integration of Mainstream and*
    Formal Epistemology 93

COLLAPSE OF DISTANCE: EPISTEMIC STRATEGIES OF SCIENCE AND TECHNOSCIENCE[1]

ALFRED NORDMANN

nordmann@phil.tu-darmstadt.de

1. Introduction

Already the title of this paper shoulders too heavy a burden of proof. By contrasting science and technoscience it alludes to an epochal break or fundamental shift in the culture of research. "Science" refers to theoretical representations of nature as we know them primarily from the history of physics and primarily from a tradition that begins with Einstein and ends with Weinberg or Hawking. It is supposed to be succeeded by technoscience, mode-2 research, post-academic, entrepeneurial, finalized, or post-normal science as we know it from pharmaceutical research, nanotechnology, ICT, and, of course, synthetic chemistry or materials research. Any such suggestion of an epochal break is vulnerable to objections. Of these, the most obvious perhaps is that there was no historical break but merely a shift of attention. Instead of focusing on the continuing inquiries by theoretical physicists and evolutionary biologists we are now foregrounding those disciplines that have always operated in a "technoscientific" or "entrepeneurial" manner (Elzinga 2002). This objection can be answered here only by suggesting that this shift of attention does not owe to the whim of historians and philosophers of science but corresponds to a shift in societal expectations and in the way researchers even at universities conceive of themselves: Chemistry and materials research have displaced theoretical physics at the pinnacle of the sciences, we increasingly look to them and the various nano-, bio-, or information technologies if we want to know what science is and does. Accordingly, the definition of "technoscience" that is operative in the following reflections does not rest on the claim that scientific practice has undergone a profound change – though, with the advent of the computer, new techniques of experimentation, visualization, and simulation there may well have been such a change, too. Instead, my definition of technoscience posits a shift in the self-understanding and epistemic values of science, adding to this only that such a shift in self-understanding will be consequential in that it serves to orient practice differently.

For the purposes of this paper, I define "technoscience" rather simply in reference to Ian Hacking's distinction of "representing" and "intervening" (Hacking 1983): *In technoscientific research, the business of theoretical representation cannot be dissociated, even in principle, from the material conditions of knowledge production* and thus from the interventions that are required to make and stabilize the phenomena. In other words, technoscience knows only one way of gaining new knowledge and that is by first making a new world.[2]

All extant definitions of "technoscience" have in common that they view it is a hybrid or monster of sorts – something that defies classification because it does not fit the classical dichotomies of nature and culture, science and technology, representing and intervening. If the business of science is the theoretical representation of an eternal and immutably given nature, and if the business of technology is to control the world, to intervene and change the "natural" course of events, we encounter the hybrid "technoscience" where theoretical representation becomes entangled with technical intervention.[3] But as soon as one encounters this hybrid technoscience and interprets it as a sign of the times, one discovers that such hybridities characterize the entire history of modern science, that nature and culture, science and technology have never been cleanly separate.[4] What appeared at first to be a hallmark of a profound transformation soon emerges as just another way of seeing the past.

Therefore, the most important words in my definition are the words "even in principle": In technoscientific research, the business of theoretical representation cannot be dissociated, *even in principle*, from the material conditions of knowledge production. Consider, for example, that 18th century theories of gases and airs referred to phenomena that were technically produced in the receiver of a vacuum pump. Even if these theories claimed to provide representations of nature, the "natural" phenomena were artificially produced. And yet, it still made sense to speak, as I just did, of natural phenomena that were technically produced. It was possible in principle and common intellectual practice to conceive of the airpump as a platform or theater that merely served as a stage where nature is prompted to act and show her tricks.[5] Conceptually, at least, scientists were able to dissociate their technical intervention from the subsequent business of producing a theoretical representation.[6] This in-principle-possibility does not obtain in the case of research with the onco mouse – to cite one of Donna Haraway's most prominent examples of technoscientific research objects (which, as we will see, should more properly be called research subjects).

A living organism that is genetically programmed to develop a certain kind of cancer differs from the airpump in that it cannot be conceived merely as a vessel in which natural processes unfold. But why not – what is the difference between airpump and onco mouse that makes the difference? Bruno Latour, Donna Haraway, Andy Pickering have a hard time answering that question and sometimes seem quite content to lump them together (Latour 1987, Haraway 1997, Pickering 1995). For the moment, a few descriptors of the onco mouse must take the place of a criterion: Onco mouse is a product of the knowledge economy, it is reproducible only to the design specifications of its distributors, it does not represent the disease process of breast cancer as it might occur in a human female but it *is* that disease process. The mouse does not exhibit a phenomenon in isolation, does not present the phenomenon as an object of learning about nature more generally. Instead of extracting general facts *from* onco mouse and then applying the lessons learned *to* humans, researchers learn to control and finally cure onco mouse as an entirely self-sufficient dynamic system. What, if anything, onco mouse models or represents therefore becomes an issue only when mouse-inquiry ends and clinical research begins, that is, when one needs to learn how to implement mouse-knowledge in a related biological system.[7]

2. Constructions of immediacy

My characterization of technoscience presented the question whether or not the animal model onco mouse represents anything, whether it is a model as models have been conceived by Heinrich Hertz or Ludwig Boltzmann and nowadays Nancy Cartwright, Margaret Morrison, or Mauricio Suárez, and others (Hertz 1956, Boltzmann 1974, Cartwright 1983, Morrison 1999, Suárez 2006).

I would like to probe more deeply at this point what the transition from classical modern science to the technosciences amounts to. I will argue that it is a transition from "artful constructions of immediacy" in modern science to a "collapse of distance" in the technosciences. This main thesis of the present discussion has a mostly critical thrust since the collapse of distance signifies methodological forgetfulness, missing critical awareness or lack of nervousness regarding reality and artefact and the limits of knowledge or control. Peter Galison refers to this as "ontological indifference" but goes on to appreciate how and why technoscience can afford such indifference (Galison 2006).

Also, we will see that the transition in question is not absolute or irreversible. Even after the collapse of distance researchers can shift perspective and re-assert the artful construction and representational rôle of a model. Indeed, the transition diagnosed here produces ambivalence and critical discussion within the scientific community itself. The traditional self-understanding of science is by no means reconciled with technoscientific practice.[8] But regardless of how conflicted individual researchers may be, the collapse of distance signals a real difficulty and calls for considerable effort to recover and reflect the artful construction of immediacy. Finally, my thesis assigns a new role to the philosophy of science. The ontological indifference of the technosciences needs to be complemented by a philosophical concern for the constructions of reality. Indeed, I hope to show that it is only through philosophical reflection that one can speak of technoscientific objectivity.

The significant step from artful constructions of immediacy to the collapse of distance involves only a small transition among the strategies required to deal with a paradoxical situation regarding representation. The very idea of representation presupposes, after all, that there is a distance between a representation and its object. This distance is that of aboutness: Our theories and representations show and tell us something *about* the world. At the same time, the acknowledgment of this distance undermines the notion that there could and should be some sort of agreement between a representation and its object. Ideally, in order to speak of "agreement" we need to conceive or construct aboutness in such manner that one can determine without artifice and mediation but somehow immediately that this statement agrees with that fact. Ideally, agreement or disagreement should be pretty much self-evident, something that we can judge by simple routines, perhaps even just by looking.[9]

This construction of immediacy is a delicate matter also in that it can go too far by collapsing the distance between a representation and its object altogether. If our representational tools become so persuasive and if we become so immersed in a representation that we take it for the thing itself, the representation ceases to be a representation and we are no longer speaking about the world but are caught up in a self-referential system.[10] Modern science and philosophy of science produced artful constructions of immediacy that maintain the aboutnes-relation if only by clearly specifying the conditions that allow us to speak of "agreement". In contrast, the collapse of distance is a hallmark of technoscience and amounts to vague and half-acknowledged epistemological confusion. While constructions of immediacy construe agreement in terms of a coordination that does not require physical similarity or a likeness between the representation and what it represents, similarity and likeness overwhelm critical distance in technoscience. It is the story of that small but significant transition which I want to outline in the following sketch. It begins – how could it be otherwise – with Immanuel Kant.

3. Representations on the battlefield of metaphysics

When Immanuel Kant began working on the *Critique of Pure Reason*, he wrote to Marcus Herz about his discovery of a new question that in his long metaphysical studies he and others "had failed to pay attention to and that, in fact, contains the key to the whole secret of hitherto still obscure metaphysics." The question was: "What is the ground of the relation of that in us which we call representation to the object?"[11]

Nine years later Kant explained in his preface to the first edition of the *Critique of Pure Reason* how the problem arose in the first place and why it has become so important to critically investigate the relation of our representations to their objects. In the course of experience arises quite unavoidably the warranted conviction that our representations usually conform to the objects: When we describe what we see, we assume safely and naturally that our descriptions agree with some object out there, namely the object we saw. Upon this conviction our reason rises "ever higher, to more remote conditions" and begins to inquire into the grounds of our conviction. How is it possible, we may ask, that our descriptions agree with some object out there? The two are of very different stuff, after all. Our descriptions take the form of thoughts or sentences and exist entirely inside our minds, while the objects are material things that exist independently in the external world, indifferent to how we think of them. Moreover, we are directly acquainted only with perceptions and sensations, with feelings and thoughts, not with the objects themselves. So, what makes us think that there can be agreement between entities as dissimilar as our representations (which we know very well because we constructed them with our own conceptual tools) and the objects (with which we have no immediate acquaintance and which we did not produce)?

It is the very success of human reason and the experience of making correct representations that gave rise to this question in the first place. But in order to answer it, reason would have to do the impossible and "surpass the bounds of all experience." It would have to step outside of human cognition and assume a divine perspective, one that would allow a direct comparison of our representations with their objects.[12] From this predicament arise profound disagreements and "the battlefield of these endless controversies is called metaphysics."[13] The combatants on this battlefield are dogmatism and skepticism.

Dogmatism here refers to a rationalism that catapults reason well beyond the bounds of experience. Indeed, it uses reason to construct a kind of divine perspective from which we can be reassured that our representations agree with the external world. The Cartesian scientist therefore begins by withdrawing from the world and in solitary meditation constructs a vantage-point for a reconstruction of how things must be. Especially in the opening of his *Meditations*, Descartes himself gave us a portrait of the investigator who beholds an object in thought such as a piece of wax. His scientific method dictates a particular way of relating to objects of acquaintance, namely by retreating from them and from a distance substituting for them a construction of the mind. If Archimedes needed to step back just far enough to unhinge the world by force of the lever, Descartes is also in need merely of a firm standpoint from which to force together by force of reason our perceptions and the external world. Accordingly he appeals to a principle of sufficient reason to argue that to differences of perception must correspond real differences of real properties. This specific argument parallels his general appeal to the benevolence of a perfect being or God who would not systematically deceive us regarding the veracity of our perceptions.[14]

While dogmatism thus employs metaphysical contrivance to force together the inner and the outer world, skepticism pries that union apart. John Locke and David Hume, in particular, showed that for all its exertions, reason cannot transcend experience but is stuck with sensory impressions. It does not achieve knowledge of causal laws, for example, because it cannot traverse the distance from the sensory experience of constant conjunctions all the way to necessary cause-effect relations. Instead, connections in the mind are forged by the sheer strength of impression. Instead of Descartes' portrait of a perfectly dissociated thinker who reinvents the world from scratch, one now gets the famous painting by Joseph Wright of Derby. It is rooted in Birmingham's Lunar Society and late 18th century British empiricism and shows the object of experience overwhelming its beholders. There is no possibility of rational ascent in the painted scene from sensory impressions to general laws. Indeed, the one experiment performed demonstrates various phenomena at once and the experiments in waiting (see the Guericke spheres on the table, the barometer, candle and

Joseph Wright of Derby (1768) *An Experiment on a Bird in the Air Pump*

watch) do not suggest a research program whereby experiments build upon each other to establish a theoretical point. And yet the experiment is compelling. In the absence of rational persuasion, what compels here is a fact so striking that it affects not only the spectators within the painting and extends to the beholder of the painting. The experiments with the airpump overwhelm the spectator, they spread enlightenment by literally displacing darkness by light (Baird and Nordmann 1994).

> This rapid process of knowledge, which, like the progress of a wave of the sea, of sound, or of light from the sun, extends itself not this way or that way only, but *in all directions*, will, I doubt not, be the means […] of extirpating *all* error and prejudice, and of putting an end to all undue and usurped authority in the business of *religion*, as well as of *science*. (Priestley 1790, xxiii)

These words of a Birmingham scientist and member of the lunar society may well serve as a description of the painting, especially its treatment of light.

They also make the Lockean point that the formation of representations is part of a natural process as impressions propagate like waves of light, leave their mark, destroy false ideas, and gradually establish the truth.

4. Artful construction

Immanuel Kant opened the door for a third approach and articulated a kind of immediacy that requires neither rational(ist) reconstructions, nor a surrender to overwhelming sensory impressions. According to Kant, dogmatism and skepticism tried to answer the wrong question by asking "Can reason bridge the gulf between our representations and their fundamentally dissimilar objects?" Between dogmatic attempts to answer yes and the skeptical reminders that the answer must be no, emerged a critical philosophy which did not provide an answer at all but removed the question: The *Critique of Pure Reason* demonstrates that there is no gulf between inside representations and outside objects. Instead of asking how our representations can agree with the objects, Kant famously proposed that we find out in which ways the objects must agree with our representations. We experience everything as given in time and space, thus susceptible to mathematical treatment. We also experience every event as the effect of a prior event and as the cause of a later event, thus susceptible to scientific or causal treatment. Time, space, causality, and other categories do not adhere to the things in themselves, they transform what is given to the senses into an object of experience that is given to the mind.

The relation between representations and their objects is thus an internal relation between entities that, far from being radically dissimilar, are actually made for each other. In a Wittgensteinian manner of speaking, what representations and their objects have in common is a grammar of construction. Ideally, this is a mathematical construction and the ideal case of agreement is therefore that between a predicted and a measured value. When Kant and his successors demand that all true science is mathematized, they privilege this quantitative agreement between numbers. Ideally again, this agreement is as immediate as the mere identity between two numbers: There is no ontological gap to be bridged and the agreement of thought and world requires neither construction nor interpretation – there is no need for a hermeneutics of science.[15]

In the history of science, hardly anyone represented this ideal as explicitly as Antoine Lavoisier who introduced precision measurement into chemistry, who transformed the chemical laboratory to the requirements of the balance

Jacques-Louis David (1788) *Portrait of Monsieur Lavoisier and his Wife*. The Metropolitan Museum of Art, Purchase, Mr. and Mrs. Charles Wrightsman Gift, in honor of Everett Fahy 1977 (1977.10). Image © The Metropolitan Museum of Art.

and the calculation of weights, and who claims to have obtained measurements that agreed to several decimal points with his theoretical predictions (Holmes 1989, see also 1985). Especially in contrast to Wright of Derby's near contemporary painting, the portrait of Lavoisier and his wife by Jacques Louis David exemplifies how a scene of representation is instituted. Since the aesthetic attitude of beholding the object is here so subtle and nuanced and involves such a precarious balancing act that it becomes clear why I should speak of an "artful" construction of immediacy.[16]

From among the many relevant differences between the two paintings I want to emphasize that in the portrait of Lavoisier the instruments are subservient to the main activity of writing and thinking. And here, the Enlightenment's light of reason takes a view from nowhere to illuminate the entire scene. Lavoisier and David show that it requires an artful construction to behold a scene in this manner. Instead of implicating and overwhelming the viewer in the violent propagation of impressions, the view from nowhere presents the scene as a scene, the object as an object, that is: from a distance. At the same time it is not dissociated from the spectator but offers this scene as one that absorbs us or holds our interest, that can be entered and explored. Where Wright of Derby's painting radiated outward, this one invites us in. But to enter this picture is a delicate and highly inferential procedure that consists in transformations of perspective that derive from and implicity preserve the rational perspective of the view from nowhere.

For example, Lavoisier is known to have transformed the laboratory by configuring it to the balance and more generally to measurement methods. Quantitative predictions could thus be confirmed by the verdict of a measurement. Therefore, aside from getting theory and experiments right, Lavoisier had to give the balance jurisdiction over chemical theories, he had to create a public space in which authority was ceded to its verdict. It no longer was to be a mere instrument for the determination of weights, nor to be vaguely associated with ideas of social or natural equilibrium. Like the scales of justice, upon weighing the evidence it would tilt to one side or the other, unambiguously determining right from wrong. In the case of chemical experimentation, it was failure to establish an equality of weight before and after a reaction which would tilt the balance against a hypothesis. Bernadette Bensaude-Vincent eloquently describes this employment of the balance:

> In the act of weighing Lavoisier sought to create an experimental space that was entirely under the experimenter's control. Once balanced with weights on Lavoisier's scale, substances were transformed from objects of nature to objects of science. The balance divested substances of their natural history. Their geographical and geological origins, their circumstances of production made little difference. They were transformed into samples of matter made commensurable by a system of standardized weights. (Bensaude-Vincent 1992, 222f.)

A seeming paradox arises from this description. Lavoisier created an experimental space "entirely under the experimenter's control," at the same time one in which the balance functioned "as an instrument of persuasion in an agonistic field." Thus, for the balance to be an instrument of persuasion the experimenters first had to persuade themselves that, for all their control, the testimony of the balance was not controlled by them at all. Bruno Latour formulates this paradox as a constitutional mandate of modern science: "[E]ven though we construct Nature, Nature is as if we did not construct it" (Latour 1993, 32). The employment of the balance in Lavoisier's new experimental space not only transformed objects of nature into objects of science, it also transformed natural historians, pharmacists, metallurgists, pneumatic chemists into that community of experimental scientists that ceded authority to the balance. In terms suggested by Michael Fried, they became absorbed into Lavoisier's experimental and rhetorical space of persuasive and arresting proof while maintaining the illusion that there is nothing theatrical about that space and that they themselves play no part in it.[17] According to the art historian Fried, the paradox of the balance (as generalized by Latour) challenged more generally the art of representation in the age of Diderot, Lavoisier, and David:

> [A] painting, it was insisted, had to attract the beholder, to stop him in front of itself, and to hold him there in a perfect trance of involvement. At the same time [...] it was only by negating the beholder's presence that this could be achieved: only by establishing the fiction of his absence or nonexistence could his actual placement before and enthrallment by the painting be secured. [...] What is called for, in other words, is at one and the same time the creation of a new sort of object – a fully realized tableau – and the constitution of a new sort of beholder – a new "subject" – whose innermost nature would consist in the conviction of his absence from the scene of representation. (Fried 1980, 103f.)[18]

As the beholders or scientific observers are drawn into the representation of nature and into a community of investigators, they become invisible to themselves and each other. Madame Lavoisier, for example, identifies her own location in the laboratory; in her drawing of experiments on respiration she is the woman to the right who is creating an objective representation of the scene. The standpoint of objectivity, however, is absent from the scene of representation, divorced from the true perspective of the observer; it is a hypothetical view from nowhere and as such a hypothetical viewpoint that can be assumed by anyone. Madame Lavoisier thus transforms her visual presence as an actor in the laboratory into an idealized absence, one that qualifies her as an invisible but objective scientific observer.[19]

By considering the art criticism of Diderot, Michael Fried shows that the balancing act between absorption and theatricality is not achieved simply by adopting the view from nowhere. In order for its beholders to willingly enter the scene and to forget its theatrical frame, the scene itself must appear unforced and "natural," corresponding to Lavoisier's emphasis on an arrangement of the givens such that we arrive at a certain conclusion through a natural chain of reasoning.

With Lavoisier and David, Latour and Fried we get a rather subtle account of scientific representation, modeling, experimentation, and objectivty. It goes

Marie-Anne Pierrette Paulze (Madame Lavoisier) (c.1793) *An Experiment on Respiration*

beyond Kant's framing in thought of the immediate internal relation of object and representation to demonstrate a specific manner of instituting this relation in the laboratory and the academy. This includes a consideration of the aesthetic and rhetorical demands upon an artlessly artful construction of a scene. As in 18th century painting, so in science: What we see must coerce or compel us without appearing contrived or forced, it needs an air of naturalness. In science, this refers primarily to the experiment as a scene that takes place in the laboratory, it might also include exhibits at a museum or the aquarium as an artificial site for a spectacle of nature, it also includes the dynamic models of Heinrich Hertz that display a behavior over time. In all these cases as in genre scenes of 18th century painting, the model or display has a reality of its own while it represents another reality. We are therefore in a state of limbo, simultaneously present and absent from that scene – its witnesses but not its creators. The human observers are silent and simply accept the verdict of nature, quite irrespective of the fact that only they have given nature the language to speak through the experiment. This dialectic of absorption and theatricality, that is, of an absorption that is theatrically produced but simultaneously negates its character as theater, is characteristic for modern science and appears in many variants.[20]

A further decisive feature of Kant's account of the construction of immediacy suggests itself here: On the one hand, the distance between representations and their objects is reduced to the immediacy of an internal relation. On the other hand, this immediacy is possible only within a critical investigation of the limits of reason. The internal relation obtains because in our thinking we cannot venture anyway beyond the phenomena to the things themselves – it obtains because we can know the world only as it is given to us and not as it is in and of itself. This, of course, is the punchline of Kant's philosophy: The limits of knowledge are constitutive of knowledge – the very idea of agreement between a representation and its object makes sense only where experience is nothing but a more less contingent system for the representation of phenomena as phenomena.

The Kantian strategy for the construction of immediacy was taken a step further by the physicist Heinrich Hertz and by Ludwig Wittgenstein. By emphasizing that the agreement between representations and their objects involves no similarity between the two, they underscore firstly Kant's focus on quantitative agreement and secondly that this agreement becomes possible only within definite limits of knowledge and language.

In the *Tractatus Logico-Philosophicus* Wittgenstein reduces the ontological gap between sentences and facts by treating sentences as facts (TLP 4.021, 2.141). A sentence is a configuration of words just like a state of affairs is a configuration of things. There is no qualitative similarity or physical likeness between these two kinds of facts, but there is a possibility of coordination that permits a simple and immediate decision regarding the agreement or disagreement between a sentence and a state of affairs. Here Wittgenstein follows Heinrich Hertz who spoke in very similar terms of the agreement between mind and world as that between two systems which model each other by way of coordination rather than physical similarity. Here is just one quote from Hertz's remarks on dynamical systems, a passage that is cited by Wittgenstein in the *Tractatus*:

> [I]t is generally impossible to carry our knowledge of the connections of natural systems further than is involved in specifying models of the actual systems. We can then, in fact, have no knowledge as to whether the systems which we consider in mechanics agree in any other respect with the actual systems of nature which we mean to be considering, than in this alone, — that the one set of systems are models of the others.
>
> The relation of a dynamical model to the system of which it is regarded as the model, is the same as the relation of the pictures our mind forms of things to these things. […] The agreement between mind and nature can therefore be compared to the agreement between

> two systems which are models of one another, and we can even account for this agreement by assuming that the mind is capable of making actual dynamical models of things and of working with them. (Hertz 1956, paragraphs 427 and 428)

The story goes on with further developments or variants to the Kantian strategy for constructions of immediacy within a framework of critical restraint. From the representatives of the Vienna Circle, in the accounts of Nelson Goodman or Donald Davidson, all the way to sociologists of scientific knowledge like Andy Pickering, one encounters expressions of the same basic idea: Once we give up all attempts to mirror the world, to reproduce in our models the exact workings by which nature effects things, we become free to make full use of our conceptual resources. By surrendering the claim that we can know how things really are, we increase our powers of representation and of creating images or theoretical models that agree with observed and measured data.

This increase in powers of representation is thus qualified by a positivist disclaimer, by an implicit and generalized footnote that accompanies all scientific work. It states that we know nothing of reality because all we have are models that are constructed by us.

5. A new animism

I would now like to contrast this positivist disclaimer of classical modern science with the animistic suggestion of technoscience: Technoscientific work is accompanied by the vague suggestion that we know everything of reality because the dynamic system in front of us is a self-sufficient reality in its own right – where this self-contained, non-referential dynamic system may be a computer simulation, a self-organizing algorithmic structure, or a model organism like the onco mouse.[21]

The positivist disclaimer consists in the qualification that all our knowledge is limited to how things appear to us in our representations. The agreement between the representation and its object or among representations allows no inference to nature as it exists beyond the constitution of objects in scientific experience. In contrast, the animistic suggestion of technoscience takes its objects as being endowed with powers that participate in the order of nature.[22] Somewhat like a voodoo doll, the onco mouse does not represent the disease process of breast cancer as it might occur in a human female but it *is* cancer or *is* the cursed object. The causal or referential connection between tumors in a onco mouse and in a diseased person remains opaque. As Donna Haraway points out, onco mouse symbolizes the patient with breast cancer such that our actions in regard to onco mouse substitute for actions in the treatment of cancer — onco mouse suffers for us and through its suffering promises healing and salvation (Haraway 1997, 79-85). In this respect still like a voodoo doll, onco mouse is not so much an object but a research subject that is vested with intentionality, it embodies the powers of cancer that are fought and must be defeated here. One works on and with it on the assumption that it simply *is* an incarnation or embodiment of cancer, and it therefore takes work to recover its representational features and to relate our mastery of this perfectly self-sufficient reality (a rodent breast cancer patient quite in its own right) to human patients or cancer in humans. Only this work of moving from one system to the next, of having to relearn mastery for each system reminds us that onco mouse might serve as a representation of sorts that establishes a correspondence of certain aspects of tumor growth in the mouse to that in humans.[23] The notion of the voodoo doll or onco mouse as a model or representation of anything is displaced and forgotten during the manipulation of the model or simulation. It needs to be actively remembered and reconstructed only as problems arise from the symbolic substitution of a dynamic system of nature by a technologically constructed dynamic system.

We may not know much about cancer, but the powers of cancer are present in the self-sufficient reality before us. Accordingly, the animistic strategy of collapsing distance replaces the immediacy of quantitative agreement between predicted and measured values by a qualitative agreement between calculated and experimental images. Their agreement consists primarily in the absence of visual clues by which to hold them apart. The technoscientific researcher frequently compares two displays or computer screens. One display offers a visual interpretation of the data that were obtained through a series of measurements (e.g., by an electron microscope), the other presents a dynamic simulation of the process he might have been observing – for this to be readable, the simulation software produces a visual output that looks like output from an electron microscope. Agreement and disagreement between the two images then allows the researchers to draw inferences about probable causal processes and to what extent they have understood them.

This story of qualitative agreement or symbolic substitution warrants closer scrutiny regarding the loss of aboutness and the entanglement in similarities. Here, the "construction of immediacy" effects only the immediacy while its constructedness within the limits of language and knowledge drops from sight.

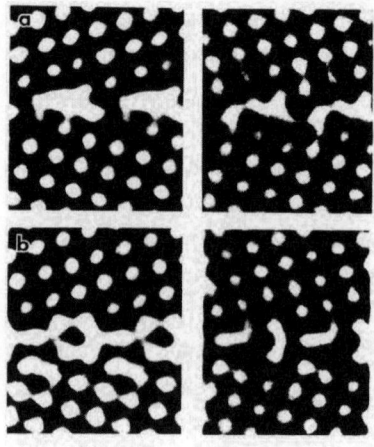

Experimental and calculated images of atoms at the grain boundaries in two structures (Merkle and Smith 1987)[24]

Thus, the relation of aboutness collapses entirely and there appears nothing arbitrary, conventional, or hypothetical about the relation between calculated and experimental images. Accordingly, the contrast between artful and deliberate constructions of immediacy and collapse of distance can be summarized (or: caricatured) as follows:

I. In classical modern science (vaguely characterized by transcendental, empiricist, or positivist attitudes), nature was explained by way of conceptual or mental constructions that, qua constructions, were well-understood – but because they were such rational constructions that relied merely on coordination with real systems, scientists found it difficult to believe that this is how things really are. Thus, when 19th century chemists used stick-and-ball models to represent molecular structure, they were extremely aware of the crude and obvious constructedness of their models, and therefore thought of them as mere didactic tools that need to be disssociated from any implied realism (Meinel 2004). Further, since they did not assume that anything corresponds to the internal machinery of explanatory models, scientists became increasingly aware of their contingency: other models might work, too, as long as they generated predictions with equal success. Philosophy of science tended to strengthen this sense of contingency by attempting to explain the success of science on the weakest possible assumptions.[25]

II. In the technoscientific "animistic" employment of computer simulations, animal models, algorithmic structures, and other substitutive uses of dynamic systems, those systems can be controlled without an understanding of their construction. This is evidenced quite simply by the fact that their scientific users do not actually make the requisite hard and software (and for the most part would not know how to make it). Rather than explicitly represent other ("real") systems by way of a specifiable coordination with them, they are symbolic substitutes for these, and the substitution includes the dynamic features that make the "real" system real.[26] When the system under study (the onco mouse, the computer simulation) refers to another system of interest (the human cancer patient, the molecular process), what distinguishes these two systems is not their reality or lack thereof. They are tangible, complete onto themselves (discrete worlds with their internal dynamics), they are experientially rich, textured or "thick," and not at all schematic. Their intimation of reality is underscored by the fact that technoscientific images tend to look alike, without visual markers to distinguish models, simulations, and real experiments. In addition to the black-boxed character of the imaging tools and the reality of the dynamic processes internal to the imaged systems, these systems can't be understood as representations because they are opaque for reasons of complexity. The system is opaque to its users for the same reason that it was developed in the first place as a self-sufficient substitute for the "real" system, namely because the real systems are too complex to be understood by the cognitive means available to humans. Instead of "understanding" in the manner of referring intellectually tractable particulars to general concepts, technoscience acquires a feeling for the system's behavior, probes its sensitivities to parameter variations, and the like, then transfers this knowledge as best one can from the isolated model systems to the integrated "real" systems.[27] For an example that updates the 19th century stick-and-ball constructions, today's molecular modeling software offers an interactive, seemingly cinematic journey into the inside of a molecule. Here, one finds it difficult to believe that what one sees might not be reality pure and simple.

This idealized contrast between classical and technoscientific models was anticipated in 1905 by Ludwig Boltzmann when he distinguished between the theoretical models of physics and the scale models of engineering.[28] The former serve constructions of immediacy along the lines suggested by Hertz. Through appropriate coordination we can determine unambiguously that this is a model of that (and vice versa). This determination, in turn, holds within set limits of knowledge that preclude us from knowing anything about the similarity between the model that serves as representation and the object that is modeled. In contrast, the scale models of engineering rely strongly on similarity. Paradoxically perhaps, for all their apparent likeness they do not permit an unambiguous, unmediated decision regarding their agreement or disagreement with situations in the world. This is not only because these can agree only in selected respects that require specification.[29] This is also because they need to be corrected for scaling effects – in order to preserve physical truth one cannot simply scale down uniformly but must introduce distortions that compensate for the scaling effects. For example, to construct a scale model of a ship in a harbor, one needs to scale down the water (and its waves) as well as the size of the ship. But in order to get the resistance of the ship right, the size of the ship needs to be factored differently than its velocity, they can't be diminished on the same scale – the ship in the model must be relatively larger.[30] Here, then, the very intimation of realism can work against the reliability and robustness of the model, and demands critical scrutiny. Engineers or technoscientists engaged in scale modeling pay attention to the ways in which a model becomes fitted, calibrated, or tuned to reality. This process can but need not involve a reconstitution of the aboutness-relation, now in highly contextualized, localized, qualitative terms.[31] Under the aegis of ontological indifference and the new animism, simulations are frequently tuned to agree with visualizations of data primarily to produce a compelling visual argument for the notion that simulation and observation partake in a shared underlying dynamics and that therefore one can substitute for the other.

Another pertinent distinction was introduced more recently by Rom Harré. Leaving aside conceptual or theoretical models altogether, he contrasts scientific instruments that serve as probes into causal processes with modeling apparatus (including simulations) that domesticates or produces phenomena. Instruments typically obtain measurements that can be traced back down a causal chain to some physical state, property, or process. As such, the instruments are detached from nature – measurements tell us something *about* the world. Physical models, in contrast, are part of nature and exhibit phenomena such that the relevant causal relations obtain within the apparatus and the larger apparatus-world complex. Whether it domesticates a known phenomenon like the rainbow or elicits an entity or process that does not occur "naturally," it does not allow for straightforward causal inference to the world within which the apparatus is nested (Harré 2003, p. 33 et passim). As the metaphor of domestication and Harré's conception of an apparatus-world complex suggest, such a causal inference from the apparatus to the world may be required only for special theoretical purposes that are characterized by a concern for reality. In the meantime and for most practical purposes, the very fact that the apparatus *is* nested in the world underwrites a continuity of principles and powers and the affordance of ontological indifference.[32]

Boltzmann, Harré, and the current proposal drive a wedge between theoretical understanding through artful coordination of detached models and animistic control by way of substitution of one bit of reality by another. This juxtaposition is epistemologically significant but its significance is normally visible only from one side of the divide, namely from the point of view of a positivist concern or apprehensiveness regarding reality, but not immediately from the point of view of an ontologically indifferent animism.[33] This indicates a new task for the philosophy of science.

Even where it sets out to better understand how technoscience achieves robust knowledge, the philosophy of science must do battle against the models and images of technoscience by making explicit their implicit claims to represent and by showing where these claims run into difficulty. It is too easy, of course, to view the collapse of distance as merely deficient in comparison to the highly self-aware and artful procedures of classical modern science and its hyperbolic self-image as rigorously anti-metaphysical. Clearly, technoscientific practice deserves a rich account of "evidence for use" and perhaps its own theory of confirmation.[34] But it is an important feature of technoscientific research that it does not seek methodological self-awareness – even if it remains incomplete without it. It is thus left to the philosophy of science to restitute and make subject to critical deliberation the aboutness-relation, the representation *and* its object *and* their relation. It is in this sense that without philosophy of science there is no technoscientific objectivity.[35]

6. Technoscientific objectivity

The problem of objectivity is solved by the artful constructions of classical modern science. Here, the object is constituted as an object of experience and something like the agreement *among* our representations *of* the object is normally taken as sufficient for the achievement of objectivity. With the collapse of distance and thus of the aboutness-relation, technoscientific objectivity requires a philosophical impulse that prompts a shift in the beholder, namely a shift from immersion within a substitute reality to absorption in a constructed scene.[36]

In order to elaborate this last point, the technoscientific manner of beholding its subjects needs to be compared to the three portraits of scientists at their business of representation by Descartes, Wright of Derby and Jacques-Louis David. I have shown how each of these three portraits responds to a problem of representation and that this is problem is shared by scientists and artists: If only God or reason can vouchsafe the agreement of thought and world, how far do we need to step back in order to reconstruct what is right in front of us? In the absence of an inferential ascent, are impressions strong enough to establish the truth? Once we have the laboratory as a theater of proof, how can we ensure that the laboratory phenomena appear natural rather than constructed? Each of these questions and the responses to them characterize a culture of representation and its institutions of specific modes of beholding. This wider cultural context is particularly apparent in the way in which technoscience beholds the world, rather: interacts with it – for here, the characteristic mode of beholding has been instituted in the immersive and substitutive aesthetics of video games.

The transition from artful constructions of immediacy to collapse of distance corresponds aesthetically to the transition from absorption to immersion. When one becomes absorbed into a scene (as described above with reference to Michael Fried), one remains a spectator of that scene, indeed one can only become absorbed on the condition that one doesn't claim any presence in the scene. Immersion, in contrast, abandons the spectatorial perspective but claims a physical presence in the midst of things. It does not assume a view from nowhere but demonstrates that it can go everywhere. The observer is the camera and the camera is the observer that performs a fly-through of a landscape, that looks from the inside-out just as easily as from the outside-in. There is no privileged vantage point, only pictures referring to other pictures.

Wolfgang Heckl is one of Germany's best known nanotechnology researchers, director of the esteemed Deutsches Museum for the history of technology, and a hobby artist who engages in molecular painting (Heckl 2003). Looking for a contemporary equivalent to Wright of Derby's or David's portraits of science, one might take this self-portrait of a nanoscale researcher as it appears on Heckl's website.

Direct molecular writing

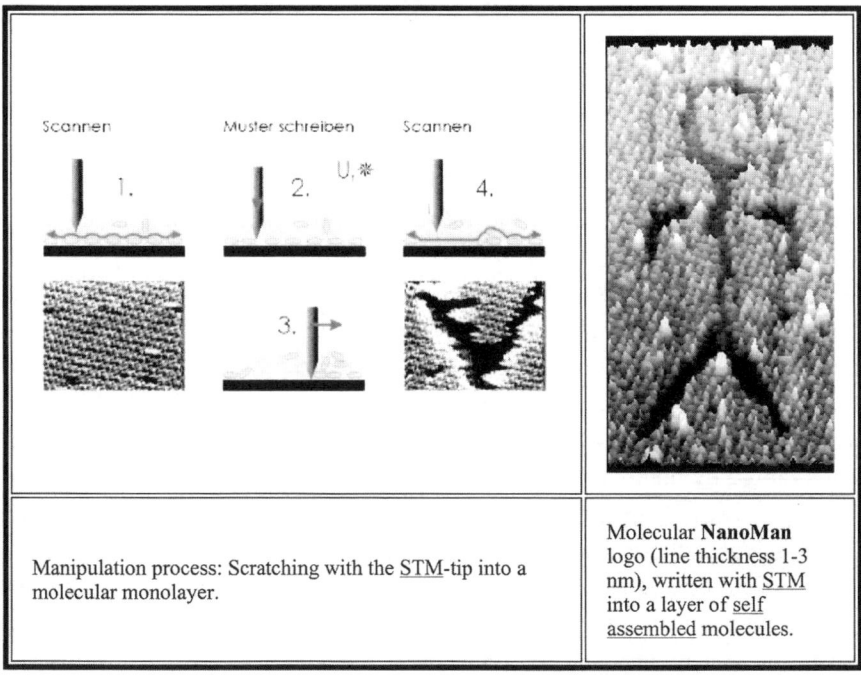

| Manipulation process: Scratching with the STM-tip into a molecular monolayer. | Molecular **NanoMan** logo (line thickness 1-3 nm), written with STM into a layer of self assembled molecules. |

Adapted from the webpage of the Scanning Probe Microscopy Group (Prof. Wolfgang Heckl) at the Ludwig-Maximilians-Universität (LMU), Munich www.nano.geo.uni-muenchen.de/external/ research/ topics/Nanomanipulation/structuring_STM/ molecular_writing/molecwrite.html (accessed December 29, 2006)

Three images add up to a bigger picture on this page. There is the schematic of a technique, an image obtained with this technique, and a videoclip that dramatizes and idealizes the process. Indeed, the videoclip provides an aesthetic standard or norm for the perfection of control that ought to be achieved at the nanoscale, namely the production of straight lines, right angles, and the like. However, the portrait of NanoMan is less than perfect and falls short of this norm (Nordmann 2006). Taken together, the three pictures serve not as the representation of some state of affairs but as a demonstration of capability. They lack an aboutness-relation as it obtains between a representation and its object, and they are clearly not images *of* a human being, *of* a molecular landscape, *of* an STM-tip, or *of* a writing tool.[37] Instead, they partake in the constitution of an object, partake in natural processes, partake in a culture of producing images just like these (including the popular practice of writing on the nanoscale the names and logos of laboratories and universities), and they partake in a general exchange or circulation of pictures that strive for photographic objectivity (full bodied, continuous, colored objects).

It remains for a more detailed analysis to show how the immersive character of these images is related to the new animism postulated above. Just one hint must suffice here: It concerns the surrender of the view from nowhere and the identification of the "observer" with the "eye" of a virtually or actually moving camera. This fusion of the observer with the moving camera produces a loss of proportion. As Felice Fraenkel has pointed out, pictures of the nanoscale are aesthetically powerful in part because we cannot tell by looking at them just how big or small things are – we are to be unmoored by them and this is one way in which they serve as "destabilizing stabilizers" (Frankel 2004, Kaiser and Mayerhauser 2005). These images demonstrate the powers of nanotechnology by demonstrating its power of visualizing what no one has seen before. The beholders of these images are in awe, reminded that "any sufficiently advanced technology is indistinguishable from magic" (Clarke 1962). With central perspective they are also abandoning a classical position of power from which the world becomes transparent and proportionate to human interests and needs. Instead, the immersed beholders of technoscientifc visualizations are surrendering to a "reenchantment of the world through technology." This return to a magical relation to the world (paradoxically, through the rational and rationalizing means of technology) is a hallmark not only of technoscience but also of the new animism.

7. Conclusions

In conclusion, I have arrived at a point where an investigation from the inside of technoscientific research joins up with outside public perspectives on technoscience. The opacity of the aboutness-relation, of visualization tools, of epistemic standards and ontological concerns corresponds to an attitude of wonder at the accomplishments of technoscience. Rather than insist on technology that rationalizes the world and enhances control, the public is left with marveling at where technoscience can go, what it can visualize, and all that it effects.

It is not at all obvious that these perspectives join up. In order to explain this, the investigation would have to go on and show that researchers and the public are in not at all dissimilar positions towards the artefacts that surround them, the tools they use, the networks of credulity and trust they rely on.

In the meantime, the claim of a new animism is bound to appear exaggerated at best, wholly inappropriate at worst. Surely, our control of phenomena in the natural world is more robust than the manipulation of a voodoo doll, even if we cannot dissect its complexity into a fully detailed causal story. And this is surely because the components of which we build our technoscientific voodoo dolls partake in the real dynamics of our natural world in a much deeper, more sustained way: These components, after all, are tried and true algorithms that have been developed in scientific contexts, that belong to established theoretical frameworks and tool-kits. Again, there is more of the story to be told here, namely how an assemblage of such robust components achieves a robustness of its own. Here, the focus was on the limits of understanding, the systematic neglect of the aboutness relation, the disappearance and thus the need for recovery of the object in technoscientific objectivity.

Notes

1. This is the revised version of a plenary lecture at the annual meeting of the Danish Philosophical Association Copenhagen, March 2006.
2. This, for example, would be a typical definition of "nanoscience" which justifies the label "nanotechnoscience": "Nanoscience studies effects that can be produced at the nanoscale and, in particular, the surprising novel properties of nanoscale materials and artefacts." – For a more elaborated characterization of technoscience see Nordmann 2004.
3. Andy Pickering explores this entanglement as a *Mangle of Practice* (Pickering 1995).
4. This is particularly evident in the title of Donna Haraway's book that revisits the "modest witness" of 17th century gentlemanly science at the end of the second millenium (Haraway 1997).
5. According to Joseph Priestley, "the experiments by the air pump, condensing engine and electrical machine […] exhibit the operations of nature and the nature of God himself" (Priestley 1761, pp. 27f.). John Robison remarks about these experiments: "We are now admitted into the laboratory of nature herself, and instructed into some of those great processes by which the author of this fair world makes it a habitable place" (Robison 1803, p. 1 vi).
6. The conviction that this distinction can be made, in principle and if only with the help of sophisticated methodological reasoning, still underwrites Nancy Cartwright's account of nature's capacities and the exhibition of concrete causal processes (Cartwright 1989).
7. To be sure, the genetic designers of onco mouse know precisely how it does and does not represent the genome of human breast cancer patient. However, the tools of technoscience are opaque even to their users. I will talk below about the work it takes for researchers to recover this information and thus to re-establish the animal model as a representational device. – If in technoscientific research one cannot, in principle, distinguish between representation and intervention, wouldn't that apply also to classic basic research like Mendel's pea-experiments? I cannot anticipate how many such "counterexamples" might be produced but this one is not compelling: Quite like the airpump that serves as a stage for the exhibition of natural phe-

nomena, Mendel's field exhibits a statistical phenomenon (even though, indeed, the individual plants are products inextricably of nature and human craft).
8. This ambivalence often takes the following form: Though they no longer insist on maintaining the difference between representing and intervening and though they acknowledge the increasing proximity of their research with engineering and design practices, scientists still claim for themselves the title of "basic researchers" who creatively go where their intellectual interests take them.
9. In 1915, Danish philosopher Harald Høffding distinguished between "visualist" and "motorist" philosopher-scientists (see Lützen 2005, p. 188). Heinrich Hertz and, of course, Ludwig Wittgenstein belong to the former group. Their account of models, images, representations is geometrically inspired and shows how one can immediately see that this agrees with that, compare Nordmann 2005b from which sections 3 and 4 below are adapted.
10. Mauricio Suárez draws on art theorist Ernst Gombrich to reflect upon this: "Gombrich employs the analogy of a hobby horse, which children play with in a similar substitutional fashion. [...] In these activities children can sometimes lose track of the fictional nature of the entity – in fact there is a sense in which for it to perform its function correctly, it is essential that the fictional nature of the entity be in some ways suppressed. Although in substitutional representation we are not required to gain the (false) belief that the fictitious entity itself exists, it seems that we are required to display at least some attitudes towards the fiction that we would display towards the real entity" (Suárez 2006, see Gombrich 1984). Suárez's account of scientific practice suggests that there is a proper (artful) attitude towards a model: While suppressing to some extent its fictional nature, scientists will not mistake it for reality. Here, I argue that this balance is easier to lose and more difficult to regain in technoscientific practice.
11. The letter dated February 21, 1772 is quoted in Paul Guyer and Allen Wood's introduction to their edition of *The Critique of Pure Reason* (Kant 1997, pp. 47f., compare A58 in the *Critique*).
12. It is a recurring theme in Kant's philosophy that such a (divine) intelligence might be possible and superior to human understanding that "requires images" (Kant 2000, paragraph 77).
13. This quotation and the preceding paraphrase come from the very first paragraphs of the first edition of Kant's *Critique of Pure Reason* (Kant 1997).
14. For a less caricatured, more faithful and appropriately detailed account see Gaukroger 2002.
15. For the need to keep interpretation out of science, see the Hobbes-Boyle dispute as reconstructed by Shapin and Schaffer 1985. More below on the historical fact that, of course, the intended exclusion of dissension and interpretation never worked, that predicted and measured values "agree" only approximately, that an interpretation of data is always necessary, and that this recognition requires a different, hermeneutic philosophy of science.
16. For a more extensive treatment of ths balancing act see Nordmann 2005a. It shows how the scientist Lavoisier and the painter David confront (and solve) a specific problem of representation.
17. In Priestley's culture of research (as depicted by Wright of Derby) it was not necessary to maintain such an illusion: Overwhelmed by experimental evidence we are swept away and deprived even of the opportunity to ask about its theatricality.
18. Fried's work is controversial among art historians because he fails to persuade that the paintings of the period actually respond to this problem. For the present purpose it is enough to agree that Fried has identified a problem of representation as it was formulated in that period.
19. In her interpretation of this drawing by Madame Lavoisier, Lissa Roberts draws on Fried's *Absorption and Theatricality* and refers to Diderot's notion of the 'pregnant moment' (Roberts 1991, 111f.). I am here following further down the tracks that were laid by her.

20. See, for example, discussions by Eric Winsberg and Mauricio Suárez of fictions in model-construction (Winsberg 2003, for Suárez see note 10 above).
21. I am here listing three candidates for more detailed case studies (or reviews of case studies). Perhaps one can add to this list uncontrolled field experiments, the visualizations obtained by scanning tunneling microscopy, etc.
22. The term 'animism' was suggested to me by Mikael Hård. I hope that it will make increasingly good sense as I go along.
23. The most superficial and powerful indicator of the tenuously representational character of animals models comes from pharmaceutical research and the large failure-rate as one moves from animal testing to clinical trials.
24. This fairly early example is indicative also of the fact that such qualitative comparisons require considerable sophistication and power of judgement: "This procedure gives reasonably good agreement between experimental and calculated images. However, minor differences, particularly in the appearance of the open spaces at the core, can be noted and will be discussed below." This eludes typical classical conceptions of modeling (in terms of coordination, projection, fitting) and challenges epistemology to make sense of statements like the following: "Atomic models which are consistent with these observed images can be verified by comparison with image simulations" (Merkle and Smith 1987, 2888).
25. This "minimalist" philosophy of science was deductivist or syntactic and remained ontologically agnostic – because it could not be ontologically indifferent, dogmatic, or skeptical. As such, it comes historically and systematically before the semantic turn and an ontologically concerned philosophy of science that attended to miracle-barring arguments and debated scientific realism.
26. The term "symbolic" is adequate in the ethnographic context since the notion of symbolic substitution agrees with the designation of this practice as a kind of animism. However, in terms of Peirce's distinction between iconic, indexical, and symbolic signs, the classical models appear indexical (by way of more or less rigid coordination) and the technoscientific dynamic systems iconic (the signs are thought to share features with the signified). For example, if the observed complexity can be modeled in terms of non-linear complex dynamics as a self-organizing system, the "power" of self-organization is thought to be equally present in (or shared by) the computer simulation and the referenced "real world situation" – even if this attribution is intractable. (The priests "know" that what they are doing to the voodoo doll they are doing also to the person for which the doll serves as a symbolic substitute – but this joint participation in a single underlying regime of powers is not transparent to them.)
27. Johannes Lenhard has focused on this limit to human understanding conceived as tracking through a system of calculations causal mechanisms or the effects of parameter variations (e.g., Lenhard 2004).
28. Boltzmann's distinction is apt, since technoscience can be characterized as (fundamental) research in an engineering or design mode.
29. Since the theoretical models of physics are constituted entirely by specifying unambiguously how their coordinates are mapped to the systems they represent, there arises for them no problem of interpretation or of identifying the relevant aspects of similarity and dissimilarity.
30. Compare Nancy Cartwright's *How the Laws of Physics Lie*: "Adjustments are made where literal correctness does not matter very much in order to get the correct effects where we want them; and very often […] one distortion is put right by another. That is why it often seems misleading to say that a particular aspect of a model is false to reality: given the other constraints that is just the way to restore the representation" (1983, 140).
31. This refers again to the "hermeneutic" approach by Nancy Cartwright and others that view

models as mediators (Cartwright 1983, 1990, Morgan and Morrison 1999, see Nordmann forthcoming). These accounts of modeling were offered to reconstruct the practice of classical modern science and thus to undermine idealized Hertzian or deductivist conceptions. If these accounts apply also to Boltzmann's engineering models this would suggest that there is perhaps no difference between scientific and technoscientific modeling, after all (this has been argued by Carrier 2004a). However, it is one thing to expose all of the work that goes into artful constructions of immediacy, and quite something else to undo a technoscientific collapse of distance in order even to recover the problem of representation. Moreover, it may well turn out that the details of the mediations are different when the construction aims for coordination and when it aims for substitution. This may affect the alignment between theoretical resources, paradigm engineering practices, models and devices, world, and the dynamic system under investigation.

32. As far as I can tell, Harré did not himself draw these conclusions from his analysis.
33. Remember that, according to Galison, ontological indifference is characteristic of those endeavors that are not concerned to establish what exists, that do not seek out fundamental praticles or construct a hierarchy of matter, and that do not aim for a theoretical representation or best explanation of how things are. – To be sure, as a matter of fact most researchers currently inhabit both sides of the divide. Cognizant of the tension, many worry about the new animism.
34. "Confirmation" may be a misleading term, suggesting as it does some formal relation between theory and evidence. Instead, technoscience may need a theory of robustness. The term "evidence for use" refers to Cartwright (forthcoming) and her proposal that more work be done in this area.
35. Martin Carrier argues that technoscience does not need such outside help because it will inevitably discover its objects, its representational commitments and difficulties – just as soon as things go wrong and the tools or instruments of technoscience become subject to scrutiny (Carrier 2004b). Carrier might underestimate here just how long one can carry on without things going wrong – especially since technoscience can exploit the tremendous plasticity of its theoretical and procedural resources. This raises the question whether mistakes and failures direct technoscientific attention to underlying assumptions and causal structures, or whether they serve as a call for more tinkering and fine tuning of functional relations. The latter approach would exemplify the technoscientific sentiment that we know so much already that we will tend to get it right. This sentiment makes it quite difficult even to raise questions about current or in-principle limits of understanding and control.
36. Another approach would consist in developing an alternative conception of objectivity, one that reflects on the presence of things in the construction of material apparatus-world systems as opposed to their absence in propositional representations of the world. This alternative approach does not view the objects as "mere objects" (of discourse) but endows them with a kind of agency, including the power to validate material constructions.
37. Such images as well as simulations give us an object but that object is only what was constituted by the image, the object is not pictured but produced by the image. Indeed, some of the objects exist only for the moment that the image was made (and for the purpose of the image). Can one go as far as saying that nanoscale phenomena are made in the image of their images? For a partial elaboration of this suggestion see Nordmann 2006.

References

Baird, Davis and Alfred Nordmann (1994) "Facts-Well-Put," *British Journal for the Philosophy of Science* 45, pp. 37-77.

Bensaude-Vincent, Bernadette (1992) "The Balance: Between Chemistry and Politics," *The Eighteenth Century* 33:2, pp. 217-237.

Boltzmann, Ludwig (1974), "Model (contribution to the 1912 edition of the *Encyclopedia Britannica*)" in Ludwig Boltzmann, *Theoretical Physics and Philosophical Problems: Selected Writings*, Dordrecht: Reidel, pp. 213-220.

Carrier, Martin (2004a) "Knowledge Gain and Practical Use: Models in Pure and Applied Research," in D. Gillies (ed.) *Laws and Models in Science*, London: King's College Publications, pp. 1-17.

Carrier, Martin (2004b) "Knowledge and Control: On the Bearing of Epistemic Values in Applied Science," in Peter Machamer and Gereon Wolters (eds.), *Science, Values and Objectivity*, University of Pittsburgh Press, pp. 275-293.

Cartwright, Nancy (1983) *How the Laws of Physics Lie*, Oxford: Clarendon.

Cartwright, Nancy (1989) *Nature's Capacities and their Measurement*, Oxford: Clarendon.

Cartwright, Nancy (1999) *The Dappled World: A Study of the Boundaries of Science*, Cambridge University Press.

Cartwright, Nancy (forthcoming) "Well-Ordered Science: Evidence for Use," forthcoming in *Proceedings of the Biennial Meeting of the Philosophy of Science Association 2004*.

Clarke, Arthur C. (1962) *Profiles of the Future: An Inquiry into the Limits of the Possible*, New York: Harper and Row.

Elzinga, Aant (2002) "Redrawing Disciplinary Boundaries – but to What Degree?" in Peter Tindemans, Alexander Verrijn-Stuart and Rob Vissers (eds.) *The Future of the Sciences and the Humanities: Four Analytical Essays and a Critical Debate on the Future of Scholastic Endeavour*, Amsterdam University Press, 149-152; the more extensive version "The New Production of Particularism in Models relating to Research Policy: A Critique of Mode 2 and Triple Helix" can be found online at http://www.csi.ensmp.fr/WebCSI/4S/theme/.

Frankel, Felice (2004) *Envisioning Science: The Design and Craft of the Science Image*, Cambridge: MIT Press.

Fried, Michael (1980) *Absorption and Theatricality: Painting and Beholder in the Age of Diderot*, Berkeley: University of California Press.

Galison, Peter (2006) "The Pyramid and the Ring," lecture at the conference of the Gesellschaft für analytische Philosophie (GAP), Berlin, September 2006.

Gaukroger, Stephen (2002) *Descartes' System of Natural Philosophy*, Cambridge University Press.

Gombrich, Ernst (1984) *Meditations on a Hobby Horse*, Chicago University Press.

Hacking, Ian (1983) *Representing and Intervening*, New York: Cambridge University Press.

Haraway, Donna (1997) *Modest_Witness@Second_Millenium*, New York: Routledge.

Harré, Rom (2003) "The Materiality of Instruments in a Metaphysics for Experiments," in H. Radder (ed.) *The Philosophy of Scientific Experimentation* (The University of Pittsburgh Press), pp. 19-38.

Heckl, Wolfgang (2003) "AlphaForum (interview with Wolfgang Heckl)," broadcast of Bayerischer Rundfunk on January 29, 2003, transcript of broadcast at www.br-online.de/alpha/forum/vor0301/20030129_i.shtml (accessed December 29, 2006).

Hertz, Heinrich (1956) *The Principles of Mechanics*, New York: Dover Publications.

Holmes, Frederic (1985) *Lavoisier and the Chemistry of Life,* Madison: University of Wisconsin Press.

Holmes, Frederic (1989) *Eighteenth-Century Chemistry as an Investigative Enterprise*, Berkeley: Office for History of Science and Technology, University of California at Berkeley.

Kaiser, Mario and Torsten Mayerhauser (2005) "Destabilizing Stabilizers," presentation at the conference *Imaging Nanospace*, Zentrum für interdisziplinäre Forschung, Bielefeld.

Kant, Immanuel (1997) *Critique of Pure Reason*, Paul Guyer and Allen Wood (translators and eds.), Cambridge University Press.

Kant, Immanuel (2000) *Critique of the Power of Judgment*, Paul Guyer (translator and ed.), Cambridge University Press.
Latour, Bruno (1987) *Science in Action*, Cambridge: Harvard University Press.
Latour, Bruno (1993) *We Have Never Been Modern*, Cambridge: Harvard University Press.
Lenhard, Johannes (2004) "Nanoscience and the Janus-Faced Character of Simulations," in Davis Baird, Alfred Nordmann, Joachim Schummer (eds.) *Discovering the Nanoscale*, Amsterdam: IOS Press, pp. 93-100.
Lützen, Jesper (2005) *Mechanistic Images in Geometric Form: Heinrich Hertz's Principles of Mechanics*, Oxford University Press.
Meinel, Christoph (2004) "Molecules and Croquet Balls," in Soraya de Chadarevian and Nick Hopwood (eds.) *Models: The Third Dimension of Science*, Stanford University Press, pp. 242-275.
Merkle, K.L. and David J. Smith (1987) "Atomic Structure of Symmetric Tilt Grain Boundaries in NiO," *Physical Review Letters* 59:25, pp. 2887-2890.
Morgan, Mary and Margaret Morrison (eds.) (1999) *Models as Mediators*, Cambridge University Press.
Morrison, Margaret (1999) "Models as Autonomous Agents," in Mary Morgan and Margaret Morrison (eds.) *Models as Mediators*, Cambridge University Press, pp. 38-65.
Nordmann, Alfred (2004) "Was ist TechnoWissenschaft? – Zum Wandel der Wissenschaftskultur am Beispiel von Nanoforschung und Bionik, "in T. Rossmann and C. Tropea (eds.) *Bionik: Aktuelle Forschungsergebnisse in Natur-, Ingenieur- und Geisteswissenschaften*, Berlin: Springer, pp. 209-218.
Nordmann, Alfred (2005a) "The Passion for Truth: Lavoisier's and Lichtenberg's Enlightenments," in Marco Beretta (ed.), *Lavoisier in Perspective*, München: Deutsches Museum, pp. 109-128.
Nordmann, Alfred (2005b) *Wittgenstein's Tractatus: An Introduction*, Cambridge University Press.
Nordmann, Alfred (2006) "Vor-Schrift – Signaturen der Visualisierungskunst," in Wolfgang Krohn (ed.), *Ästhetik in der Wissenschaft: Interdisziplinärer Diskurs über das Gestalten und Darstellen von Wissen*, Hamburg: Felix Meiner, pp. 117-129.
Nordmann, Alfred (forthcoming) "'Getting the Causal Story Right': Hermeneutic Moments in Nancy Cartwright's Philosophy of Science," in Stephan Hartmann and Luc Bovens (eds.) *Nancy Cartwright's Philosophy of Science*, London: Routledge.
Pickering, Andrew (1995) *The Mangle of Practice*, University of Chicago Press.
Priestley, Joseph (1761), *Lectures on History and General Policy*. Volume 24 of J.T. Rutt (ed.), *The Theological and Miscellaneous Works of Joseph Priestley*, London, 1817-1831.
Priestley, Joseph (1790) *Experiments and Observations on Different Kinds of Air*, vol. 1, Birmingham (reprint New York: Kraus Reprint, 1970).
Roberts, Lissa (1991) "Setting the Table," in Peter Dear (ed.) *The Literary Structure of Scientific Argument*, Philadelphia: University of Pennsylvania Press, pp. 99-132.
Robison, John (1803) "Introduction," in Joseph Black, *Lectures on the Elements of Chemistry*, Edinburgh, vol. 1.
Shapin, Steven and Simon Schaffer (1985) *Leviathan and the Air-Pump*, Princeton University Press.
Suárez, Mauricio (2006) "Scientific Fictions as Heuristic Rules of Inference," unpublished presentation at the Scientific Images Symposium, American Philosophical Association, Central Division Meeting, Portland, Oregon, 25 March.
Winsberg, Eric (2003): "Simulated Experiments: Methodology for a Virtual World," *Philosophy of Science* 70, pp. 105-125.
Wittgenstein, Ludwig (1922) *Tractatus Logico-Philosophicus*, London: Routledge and Kegan Paul.

VOM JENSEITS DES BEKANNTEN.
ADORNO UBER DARSTELLUNG, SPRACHE
UND RHETORIK

MIRKO WISCHKE

Martin-Luther-Universität Halle-Wittenberg

Gibt es eine ‚Sprache' der Dinge? Was ist mit dieser Sprache gemeint? Sind es die Worte und Begriffe, mit denen wir die Dinge bezeichnen und ihnen einen Namen geben? Wenn wir aber den Dingen Namen geben und mit Begriffe bezeichnen, sind es dann nicht *unsere* Worte und Begriffe, nicht aber die der Dinge? Geht es also in unserer Sprache gar nicht um die Dinge? Ist diese Folgerung richtig, warum gebraucht Adorno dann die Formulierung von der "Sprache der Dinge" in der "Ästhetischen Theorie"?

> "Die Buchstaben, die ich gerade darauf (auf das Blatt Papier – M. W.) geschrieben hatte, waren noch nicht trocken, und schon gehörten sie mir nicht mehr."
>
> Jean Paul Sartre

Warum sollte der Autor dem Leser verweigern, Einblick in seine Gedankengänge zu nehmen? Was hindert den Autor daran, in seinen Ausführungen ein gewisses Maß an Rücksicht auf den Leser zu üben? Will er nicht von seinem Leser verstanden werden?

Adornos Kritik an die gegen den Schriftsteller gerichtete Aufforderung, seine Schritte möglichst explizit, d. h. nachvollziehbar zu machen, um den Leser in die Lage zu versetzen, die Überlegungen des Autors gedanklich nachvollziehen zu können, scheinen diese trivial anmutenden Fragen zu provozieren. Wie kann Adorno behaupten, dass die "Aufforderung, man solle sich der intellektuellen Redlichkeit befleißigen, […] auf die Sabotage der Gedanken" hinaus läuft? (Adorno 1989, S. 99) Welche Überlegungen bewegen Adorno, nicht nur zu bestreiten, dass dem Autor eine solche Aufgabe überhaupt zumutbar ist, sondern es auch als ein falsches Darstellungsprinzip zu bezeichnen, das von der "Fiktion […] der Kommunizierbarkeit eines jeden Gedankens" ausgeht? Gibt es Gedanken, die unkommunizierbar sind?

Auf diese Fragen soll im Folgenden nach Antworten gesucht werden. Dabei interessieren mich diejenigen Überlegungen, die Adorno zu der These bewegen, dass die Fiktion der uneingeschränkten Kommunizierbarkeit der Gedanken ihren "sachlich angemessenen Ausdruck" hemmt – eine These, die radikalisiert in der Formulierung zum Ausdruck kommt, dass der Wert eines Gedankens "sich an seiner Distanz von der Kontinuität des Bekannten" misst. (Adorno 1989, S. 99) Zunächst soll (*I.*) untersucht werden, was unter Distanz im Hinblick auf die Darlegungsmöglichkeit von Gedanken zu verstehen ist. Danach wird (*II.*) Adornos Hinweis auf das isolierte Dasein des Begriffs, der den Wert eines Gedankens ebenso mindert wie die fehlende Distanz, im Zusammenhang mit seinen Überlegungen zur Darstellung zu betrachten sein. Den Leitfaden dieser knappen Erörterung bildet die Ansicht, dass Adornos Kritik an der beliebigen Mitteilbarkeit von Gedanken in einer skeptischen Erkenntnistheorie wurzelt, die in denjenigen Überlegungen zum Ausdruck kommt, in denen es darum geht, dass der Begriff in einer nur sehr eingeschränkten Weise den Sachverhalt, auf den er sich bezieht, zum Ausdruck bringt. Vor dem Hintergrund der Neigung des Begriffs zur Verselbstständigung geht es (*III.*) abschließend um die Exposition der Rhetorik in Adornos Betrachtungen. Wenn dass Sein der Dinge sprachlich erschließbar ist, die Begriffe jedoch, in denen wir sprechen und denken, einen Hang zur Verselbstständigung und Objektivierung haben, geht es Adorno bei der ‚Darstellung' um das Erkenntnispotential von Sprache, das mittels einer Rehabilitierung der Rhetorik erschlossen werden soll. Meine These – die ich Ihnen erläutern möchte – geht von der Überlegung aus, dass die Rhetorik Adornos Diktum von der Unkommunizierbarkeit des Gedankens sowohl in unterschiedlicher Weise zu verstehen erlaubt als auch verstehen lässt, warum ein unkommunizierbarer Gedanke der Auslöser von Erfahrung sein kann.

I. Begriff und Erkenntnis

Ist "Sprache [...] der eigenen objektiven Substanz nach gesellschaftlicher Ausdruck" (Adorno 1989, S. 292), wie aus den "Minima Moralia" zu erfahren ist, könnte Adornos Rede von der Fiktion der Kommunizierbarkeit eines jeden Gedankens so verstanden werden, dass zur banalen Praxis des Sprachgebrauchs, in dem sich gewöhnlich Kommunikation vollzieht, auf Distanz zu gehen ist, um nicht Gefahr zu laufen, komplexen Gedankengängen ihre Schärfe und Substanz zu rauben. "Texte, die [...] jeden Schritt ängstlich nachvollziehen, verfallen [...] unweigerlich dem Banalen" (Adorno 1989, S. 99), lautet Adornos Fazit, das er an Georg Simmel illustriert: "Die Schriften Simmels etwa kranken allesamt an der Unvereinbarkeit ihrer aparten Gegenstände mit der peinlich luziden Behandlung." (Adorno 1989, S. 100) Die Transparenz der logischen Genesis seiner Gedanken erkaufe Simmel mit der Redundanz kategorialer Formen, in denen seine scharfsinnigen Gedanken und Analysen erstarren und verloren gehen würden.

Bei einer ersten Lektüre dieser Zeilen entsteht der Eindruck, dass Adornos Urteil – das ich nicht kommentieren will – von dem Gedanken auszugehen scheint, dass der jeweils behandelte Sachverhalt einer ihm typischen sprachlichen Darstellung bedarf. Welche Herausforderung darin für den Autor liegt, lässt sich daran ermessen, dass der Sinn von Worten, der ihnen in der sprachlichen Mitteilungspraxis widerfährt, das Material des Schriftstellers ausmacht, an dem er durch die positive wie negative Valenz (Wertigkeit von Verben) der Sprache gebunden ist, um eine ihm selbst nicht völlig transparente, weil "in einem Geflecht von Vorurteilen, Anschauungen, Innervationen, Selbstkorrekturen, Vorausnahmen und Übertreibungen" gemachte Erfahrung zu artikulieren. (Adorno 1989, S. 100 f.) Diesen Aspekt beleuchtet Adorno im Abschnitt *Moral und Stil* der "Minima Moralia" mit einer Äußerung, in der ein kulturkonservatives Ressentiment zu spüren ist, behauptet er doch, dass das "vom Kommerz geprägte Wort (vertraut) berührt" (Adorno 1989, S. 128), hingegen die Gewöhnungsbedürftigkeit ungewohnter Artikulation fremd und abweisend erscheint. Der Sprachgebrauch stellt den Vorgang alltäglicher vorwissenschaftlicher Lebenspraxis dar, auf den der Schriftsteller angewiesen zu sein scheint, wenn er verstanden werden will. Geht er zu dieser Praxis auf Distanz, mindert sich das Risiko, dass seine Gedankenwerkstatt voll von umgangssprachlich verengten und entstellten Sprachformen ist, jedoch hat diese Abkehr ihren Preis. Denn "beim Ausdruck auf die Sache schauen, anstatt auf die Kommunikation, ist verdächtig: das Spezifische, nicht bereits dem Schematismus Abgeborgte erscheint rücksichtslos, ein Symptom der Eigenbrötlerei, fast der Verworrenheit". (Adorno 1989, S. 128) Obwohl es in den "Minima Moralia" wiederholt Hinweise Adornos gibt, in denen er auf diese Gefahr aufmerksam macht – mit der er mehr zu kokettieren als sie zu fürchten scheint -, lässt sich das, was er unter Distanz im Hinblick auf die Darlegungsmöglichkeit von Gedanken versteht, nicht mit diesem Aspekt ausloten. (Adorno 1989, S. 292)

In welche Dimension Adornos Verweis auf die Notwendigkeit der Distanz reicht, lässt sich erahnen, wenn er in der "Negativen Dialektik" betont, dass das Objekt der Sprache weder "reine Faktizität" noch ein bloßes Denkprodukt ist. (Adorno 1982, S. 189) Auf diese Dimension macht die Sprachtheorie aufmerksam, die Adorno mit Horkheimer in der "Dialektik der Aufklärung" entwirft; deren zentraler Kern besteht in der These, dass Sprache in dem Maße

‚verdinglicht' wird und ‚verdinglichend' ist, wie sie in Bezeichnung und Klassifikation von Gleichbleibendem überzugehen beginnt. Was Gedanken mittels Sprache zum Ausdruck bringen wollen, verhindert eine Schranke, die nicht hintergehbar ist, da nicht die Willkür menschlicher Subjekte einer angemessenen Artikulation von Sachverhalten im Wege steht, sondern die volle Erkenntnis der Dinge bereits an der Sprache selbst zu scheitern scheint. In diesem Sinne betont Adorno, dass die "Erkenntnis, die den Inhalt will, [...] die Utopie" will (Adorno 1982, S. 66), und dass die "Utopie der Erkenntnis" darin besteht, "das Begrifflose mit Begriffen aufzutun". (Adorno 1982, S. 21)

Folgt aus dieser Feststellung für unsere Ausgangsfrage, dass Gedanken eigentlich unkommunizierbar sind, da Worte nicht hinreichend erfassen können, was sie zum Ausdruck bringen sollen? Darauf scheint der Hinweis auf das *Begrifflose* am Begriff hinzuweisen, das sich der begrifflichen Vorstellungskraft entzieht und allein negativ bestimmbar ist als das, was über den Begriff hinausweist und jenseits des begrifflich Zugänglichen und Erkannten liegt. Unbefriedigend bleibt diese Folgerung, wenn man sie mit der Prämisse der Sprachtheorie der "Dialektik der Aufklärung" konfrontiert. Wenn keine genaue Entsprechung zwischen Wort und gemeinter Sache existiert, bleibt unklar, wie mittels Begriffe erfahrbar werden soll, was nichtbegrifflicher Natur ist.

Oder muss die Folgerung lauten, dass Gedanken kaum in Worte zu fassen sind, da sie eine oszillierende Bedeutungsbreite besitzen, die einen Gedanken mitteilbar zu machen waghalsig werden lassen? Das scheint der Verweis auf den *Inhalt* der Erkenntnis nahe zu legen, den die sprachlich-begriffliche *Form* der Erkenntnis insofern entgegen steht, als die Sprache unserem Denken vorausliegt. Die Sprache hat Einfluss auf unser Denken; der Mensch macht sich mit der Sprache eine Vorstellung von der Welt, "die er dann *als* Meinung über die Welt ratifiziert, sobald er in der Sprache redet und denkt". (Kopperschmidt 1994, S. 48) Ist keine genaue Entsprechung zwischen Wort und gemeinter Sache anzunehmen, bleibt unklar, gemessen an welchen Kriterien von einer gedanklichen Einsicht überhaupt die Rede sein kann.

Die Überlegung, die Adorno zu seiner Feststellung vom utopisch anmutenden Unterfangen der Erkenntnis führt, ist bereits dem jungen Hegel nicht fremd gewesen, der Kants Annahme kritisiert, dass "in allen *Subsumtionen* eines Gegenstandes unter einen Begriff [...] der Begriff [...] dasjenige enthalten (muss), was in dem darunter zu subsumierenden Gegenstande vorgestellt wird". (Kant 1990, A 137, S. 187) Wenn der Begriff bereits enthält, was der

Erkenntnisgegenstand in unserer Vorstellung darstellt, verstellen die Begriffe die wirkliche Erkenntnis dessen, was uns sinnlich gewiss zu sein scheint, anstatt sie zu ermöglichen; was wir eine Erkenntnis der Dinge nennen, beruht auf allgemeine Vorstellungen, die uns die Begriffe vermitteln. Adorno scheint Hegels Bedenken zu teilen, verweist er doch darauf, dass der Begriff der Illusion erliegt, die Sachverhalte, die er zum Ausdruck bringen soll, als Festes und Beständiges zu hypostasieren, d. h. als das, was die Sachverhalte an sich gar nicht sind.

Adornos Feststellung, der Begriff hypostasiere "seine eigene Form gegenüber den Inhalten" (Adorno 1982, S. 156), erinnert nicht nur an Hegels Beobachtung einer durch die Reflexion fixierten Entgegensetzung von Begriff und Sachverhalt als jeweils für sich bestehende Bereiche, sondern auch an Platons Einsicht in die innere Verkehrungstendenz, mit der das Wort, der Begriff, die Einsicht und die Veranschaulichung sich selbst zur Geltung zu bringen versuchen, anstatt hinter dem, was sie gegenwärtig machen sollen, zu verschwinden. Platon bezeichnet dies als die Schwäche der Sprache (*Logoi*): sich gleichsam vor das zu drängen, was sich in ihnen zeigt. Wort, Begriff, Einsicht und Veranschaulichung neigen dazu, sich als das geltend zu machen, was sie für sich sind, weil sie alle auch ein Sein für sich selber haben, durch das sie sich von dem unterscheiden, was sie als die Sache darstellen. Aus dieser Differenz erklärt sich nicht nur für Platon, sondern auch für Adorno, warum die begriffliche Erkenntnisleistung nicht darin besteht, einen Zugang zu den Dingen, wie sie wirklich sind, zu ermöglichen. Andere Autoren, wie Gadamer, ziehen aus dieser Einsicht den Schluss, dass in der Sprache, wo das Wort nicht wie ein Zeichen auf etwas anderes verweist, es nicht darum geht, die Dinge so zu erkennen wollen, wie sie wirklich sind. (Gadamer 2000, S. 205)

II. Sprache und Denken

Weder zieht Adorno einen ähnlichen Schluss wie Gadamer – auch wenn er bestreitet, dass die Sprache ein "bloßes Zeichensystem für Erkenntnisfunktionen" (Adorno 1982, S. 164), ist – noch ist er wie Nietzsche überzeugt, dass die Sprache es uns prinzipiell verwehrt, die Dinge als das zu erkennen, was sie an sich sind. Adorno bescheinigt zwar Nietzsche, als einziger dagegen aufbegehrt zu haben, dass die "Invarianz des Begriffs [...] mit der Unveränderlichkeit des Seins an sich" zu rechtfertigen ist. (Adorno 1990, S. 27) Aber er teilt nicht Nietzsches Ansicht, wonach die Wahl zwischen bloßem "für-Wahrhalten"

(Nietzsche 1988a, S. 103, 2[84]) und wirklicher Erkenntnis insofern keine Alternative ist, als davon auszugehen ist, dass es keine Erkenntnis der Wahrheit im eigentlichen Sinne gibt. Der Mensch hat keinen Zugang zu den Dingen, wie sie wirklich sind – eine Verlegenheit, die er laut Nietzsche mit der Sprache bewältigt, in der sich jedoch nicht die Bezeichnungen und die Dinge decken. Denn die Sprache stellt ebenso wenig etwas dar wie sie etwas abbildet; was sie bezeichnet, ist allein die Relation der Dinge zu den Menschen: "[…] nicht die Dinge (selbst) treten ins Bewusstsein, sondern die Art, wie *wir* zu ihnen stehen." (Nietzsche 1988b, S. 879)

Die Möglichkeit des Perspektivismus zieht Adorno nicht in Betracht. Vielmehr verkennt seine Würdigung von Nietzsches Kritik an der Metaphysik des Bleibenden als einen Beitrag zur Auflösung der "Hypostasis des Dinges" (Adorno 1990, S. 27) den eigentlichen Ansatz Nietzsches, dem es nicht um eine (zeitliche) Präsenz der Dinge im Unterschied zu deren "wahrem" Sein geht, sondern darum, dass die Metaphorizität und der Anthropozentrismus der Sprache der Selbstbehauptung des Menschen dienen, und zwar in elementarster Weise: allein in der Sprache nämlich hat der Mensch laut Nietzsche einen Zugang zur Welt (vgl. Müller-Lauter 1999); ohne die Sprache könnte er sich weder in der Welt orientieren noch sich diese verfügbar machen.

Obgleich weder Nietzsches Perspektivismus noch dessen Ansatz Anerkennung bei Adorno finden, sind ihm dessen Überlegungen insofern nicht fremd, als er erkenntniskritisch bezweifelt, dass sich ein Standpunkt außerhalb der Sprachpraxis finden lässt, von dem aus jenseits von allen sprachlichen Entstellungen die Dinge so wahrgenommen werden könnten, wie sie wirklich sind. Charakteristisch für die Sprache ist die "Inadäquanz von Gedanke und Sache" (Adorno 1982, S. 156), durch die keine Erkenntnis ihren Gegenstände ganz inne hat. Ebenso berühren sich Adornos Überlegungen mit Nietzsches Erwägungen in dem Punkt, wo dieser darauf verweist, dass allein die Sprache den Menschen einen Zugang zu der ihm umgebenen Welt gewährt und auf diese Weise unverzichtbar für das menschliche Dasein ist. Denn auch Adorno geht davon aus, dass "Sprache als Organon des Denkens" zu verstehen ist (Adorno 1982, S. 66), die Bildung von Begriffen primär zu Zwecken der Naturbeherrschung erfolgt und dass Begriffe auf "Nichtbegriffliches" verweisen (Adorno 1982, S. 23), zu dem wir keinen wirklichen Zugang haben. Nietzsches Perspektivismus reicht aber Adorno nicht aus, um zu erklären, wie die Begriffe einen Bezug zu Sachverhalten haben können, wo sie doch mit den Dingen nur in einer sehr fragwürdigen Weise übereinstimmen. Adorno begnügt sich nicht mit dieser Tatsache, an der er nicht nur einen negativen Aspekt wahrnimmt, sondern auch entdeckt, dass Begriffe, weil sie "emphatisch Nichtbegriffliches" bedeuten, über sich hinaus "meinen". (Adorno 1982, S. 23) Überzeugt, dass Begriffliches und Unbegriffliches als zwei verschiedene Bereiche nicht in ihrer Trennung absolut zu fixieren sind, ist Adorno weniger der von Kant hervorgehobene Umstand problematisch, dass zwischen Sprache und Außersprachlichem eine schier unüberbrückbare Kluft besteht. Wie Nietzsche und Gadamer geht Adorno davon aus, dass sich der Mensch die Welt einzig in der Sprache erschließt, und auch wenn die Begriffe dazu neigen, diesen Zugang zu verschütten, gehört doch "zu ihrem Sinn […], dass sie in ihrer eigenen Begrifflichkeit nicht sich befriedigen, obwohl sie dadurch, dass sie das Nichtbegriffliche als ihren Sinn einschließen, es tendenziell sich gleichmachen und damit in sich befangen bleiben". (Adorno 1982, S. 23) Begriffe neigen zur Objektivierung und Vergegenständlichung von Sachverhalten, die von sich aus weder Objekte noch Gegenstände sind.

Diese Einsicht lässt verständlich werden, warum Adorno in scheinbarer Umkehrung seiner Kritik an die Forderung nach Kommunizierbarkeit der Gedanken betont, dass der Schriftsteller in dem Maße, wie er präziser, gewissenhafter, sachlich angemessener sich auszudrücken versucht, um die Differenz zwischen Sache und Ausdruck auszulöschen, die unangenehme Erfahrung machen wird, dass sein literarisches Resultat für schwer verständlich gilt. (Adorno 1989, S. 128) Lässt sich aber diese Differenz überhaupt tilgen? Und ist es überhaupt sinnvoll, versuchen zu wollen, diese Differenz zu auszulöschen?

In dem Abschnitt der "Minima Moralia", der den Gegenstand meiner Ausführungen bildet, ist die Antwort auf diese Fragen mit einer gewissen Melancholie behaftet, da "jedem Gedanken […], der nicht müßig ist, […] wie ein Mal die Unmöglichkeit der vollen Legitimation einbeschrieben (bleibt), so wie wir im Traum davon wissen, dass es Mathematikstunden gibt, die wir um eines seligen Morgens im Bett willen versäumten, und die nie mehr sich einholen lassen". (Adorno 1989, S. 101) Wie vermag Sprache an Gedachtes heranzureichen, wenn doch die Sprache das Denken vorschreibt und dergestalt eine Legitimation des Gedankens behindert, wenn nicht gar verhindert und vielleicht sogar unmöglich macht?

Ausgehend von der Annahme, dass jede Erkenntnis eine *"Erkenntnis durch Begriffe"* ist (Kant 1999, B 93, S. 109), hat Kant bekanntlich die Einschränkung gemacht, dass Begriffe sich niemals unmittelbar auf einen Gegenstand beziehen; den Begriffen liegen keine "Bilder" der Gegenstände zugrunde;

Denken ist nichts anderes als die Erkenntnis durch Begriffe: Die reinen Verstandesbegriffe liefern "*keine Erkenntnis von Dingen*". (Kant 1999, B 148, S. 146) Hegel stimmt Kant nicht nur darin zu, dass die Begriffe ihre eigene Wirklichkeit konstituieren; in der "Phänomenologie des Geistes" radikalisiert er diese Einsicht zu der Annahme, dass das unmittelbare Sein nicht sprachlich zum Ausdruck gebracht werden kann. Aufgrund dieser unhintergehbaren Grenze der Sprache ist es letztlich "gar nicht möglich, dass wir ein sinnliches Sein, das wir *meinen*, je sagen können", da der Begriff in etwas anderem als der sinnlichen Wirklichkeit existiert. (Hegel 1973, S. 85)

Dieser Annahme stimmt Adorno insofern zu, als er behauptet, dass "Sprache [...] das Auszudrückende auf ein je schon Vorgegebenes und Bekanntes vermöge ihrer Allgemeinheit" nivelliert (Adorno 1974, S. 477), und er das "Nichtidentische (als das) [...] von seiner Allgemeinheit Unterschiedene, Differenziertere" definiert (Adorno 1990, S. 27), ohne sich Hegels These verpflichtet zu fühlen, dass in der sprachlichen Repräsentation *generell* nicht das Gemeinte als das unmittelbare sinnliche Sein zum Ausdruck kommt, sondern das Einzelne in der Form des Allgemeinen ausgesprochen wird, obwohl wir uns dabei das allgemeine Sein überhaupt nicht vorstellen. Kants Ansicht, dass die Begriffe, indem sie unterschiedliche Ansichten zu einer allgemeinen Vorstellung ordnen, eine Kenntnis von Dingen durch allgemeine Vorstellungen sind (Kant 1961, S. 42), bildet das theoretische Fundament von Hegels Überzeugung, dass das, was wir vom sinnlichen Sein sagen, von der sinnlichen Wirklichkeit unterschieden ist. (Vgl. Englisch 1990) Diese erkenntnistheoretische Prämisse teilt Adorno, auch wenn er Hegels Gedankengang mit einem Zusatz versieht: Dass unser Denken von Sprache abhängig ist, versteht Adorno in der Weise, dass "der Begriff [...] in ein nichtbegriffliches Ganzes verflochten ist, gegen das er durch seine Verdinglichung einzig sich abdichtet, die freilich als Begriff ihn stiftet". (Adorno 1982, S. 24) Hegels Prämisse trifft für Adorno nicht generell auf *die* Sprache zu, sondern beschreibt das Phänomen der Objektivierung nichtobjektivierbarer Sachverhalte in der Sprache. Wie Nietzsche und Gadamer in ihren Überlegungen zur Sprache Abschied von einer Ontologie des Vorhandenen nehmen, in der Überzeugung, dass die Existenz eines Wortes *nicht* mit der Existenz des damit bezeichneten Sachverhaltes gleichzusetzen ist, vertritt auch Adorno die Ansicht, dass der *Gebrauch* der Sprache nicht mit dem gleichzusetzen ist, was in ihr eigentlich zur Sprache kommen soll: dem Nichtbegrifflichen, das im Begriff durch seine Bedeutung überlebt, auf die sich das Begriffsein des Nichtbegrifflichen gründet. Im Unterschied zu Gadamer, für den nicht die Frage das eigentliche Problem ist, wie wirklichkeitsnah oder -fern die Dinge zur Sprache gebracht werde, und im Gegensatz zu Nietzsche, für den der pragmatische Aspekt von Sprache letztlich am bedeutsamsten ist, besitzt die Sprache für Adorno eine wirkliche Erkenntnisbedeutung – auch wenn in seiner Perspektive das Sein des Wortes nicht in seiner Bedeutung aufgeht.

Ohne Frage ist Gadamer im Recht, wenn er darauf verweist, dass die "Vorbekanntheit des zu Bezeichnenden vor aller Bezeichnung [...] nicht der Fall von Sprache" ist. (Gadamer S. 101) Allerdings würde Adorno hinzufügen, dass das Bezeichnete – das Vorsprachliche – lediglich einseitig, fragmentarisch, rudimentär und verstümmelt zur Sprache kommt, weil seine Funktion mit dem Imperativ der Naturbeherrschung abgestimmt ist. Was Nietzsche als anthropologisch unhintergehbares Übel betrachtet, wendet Adorno zu der Frage nach der Möglichkeit, wie mittels der Sprache die Schranken der Sprache durchbrochen werden können, um das in den Blick zu bekommen, was die scheinbare Identität von Begriff und Sache – die bereits Platon im Dialog "Kratylos" auf ihre Stimmigkeit untersucht – dementiert: das, was Sprache nicht sagt, obwohl es ihr vorausgeht und die Sprache sich darauf bezieht: das Nichtsprachliche, Nichtbegriffliche, Nichtidentische. Die Frage ist, wie Sache und Ausdruck mit den Mitteln der Sprache zusammenrücken können, wenn es doch das Prinzip der Sprache sein soll, sich gegenüber dem Auszudrückenden zu verselbstständigen. Konkretisiert auf den von mir untersuchten Abschnitt der "Minima Moralia" lautet die Frage: Wie kann vom unkommunizierbaren Nichtsprachlichen bzw. Nichtbegrifflichen Wahres erkannt werden, wenn die Form der Erkenntnis (und Mitteilung) sprachlich-begrifflicher Natur ist?

Man könnte meinen, eine hinreichende Antwort auf diese Frage in Adornos Behauptung von der inneren Transzendenz des Begriffs, die diesem durch seinen Bezug auf Nichtbegriffliches eigen ist, zu finden. Doch wie ist etwas in Begriffen darstellbar, worauf sich die Begriffe beziehen, ohne es doch aus eigener Kraft zur Darstellung bringen zu können? Die vorläufige Antwort lautet: Durch die Darstellung, die keine Repräsentation im Sinne einer kognitiven Vorstellung ist, sondern eine eigene Form, die etwas hervorbringt, (Scholze 2000, S. 299) an dem Autor wie Leser teilhaben. Unklar ist vorerst noch, welche Kriterien die Darstellung erfüllen muss, um im Begrifflichen Nichtsbegriffliches transformieren zu können. Man kann die Frage auch so stellen: Wie ist es möglich, die Schwäche der Begriffe, sich vor das zu stellen, was sie doch eigentlich ausdrücken sollen, zu überwinden? Wie können Begriff und Sache ihre Differenz minimieren, ohne sie doch gänzlich abschütteln?

III. Darstellung und Rhetorik

Eingebunden in die jeweilige Sprache der Darstellung werden die Begriffe gleichsam verflüssigt, indem sie in Konstellationen sich gruppieren, um an ihnen das gewahr werden zu lassen, was die Begriffsschemata verdecken. Allein die Darstellung in Form solcher Begriffskonstellationen repräsentiert, was das Material, der "Begriff im Innern weggeschnitten hat, das Mehr" am Begriff. Dass die Darstellung der Konstellation der "Intention des Begriffs, das Gemeinte ganz auszudrücken" (Adorno 1982, S. 164), dient, führt Adorno darauf zurück, dass die Begriffe, indem sie sich "um die zu erkennende Sache [...] versammeln", denkend erreichen, was begriffliches "Denken aus sich notwendig ausmerzt". (Adorno 1982, S. 165) Offen bleibt, wie der Rückgang der Begriffe auf Sprache zu denken ist. Offensichtlich meint Adornos, dass das Verhältnis, in das die Form der Konstellation die Begriffe in der Darstellung setzt, um sie um eine Sache zu zentrieren, bereits als Sprache zu bezeichnen ist, wenn er Sprache und Darstellung ineins setzt. (Adorno 1982, S. 164) In wechselhaften Gruppierungen um einen Sachverhalt fokussiert, sollen die Begriffe jene sprachliche Vieldeutigkeit rückgewinnen, die sie als Gesprochene im Vollzug der Sprache haben. Diese Rückgewinnung veranschaulicht Adorno an jener Passage der Odyssee, wo der gleichnamige antike Held in der Höhle des Zyklopen "erfährt, dass das identische Wort Verschiedenes zu bedeuten vermag". (Adorno/Horkheimer 1987, S. 84)

Die Rückgewinnung der sprachlichen Vieldeutigkeit ist jedoch nur ein erster Schritt. In Annäherung an das gesprochene Wort soll der Begriff nicht nur die Vieldeutigkeit wiedererlangen, die erst der Stellenwert, den er im Zusammenhang der jeweiligen Rede besitzt, mindert; es soll auch das begriffliche Identifikationsprinzip aufgebrochen werden, um dem nichtbegrifflichen Sinn des Begriffs gewahr zu werden, den die Form der Konstellation zu einer vorläufigen Darstellung kommen lassen soll.

Die Wiedereingliederung der Begriffe in Sprache, die Erinnerung an die sprachliche Form der Begriffe ist der Versuch, das mimetische Potential der Sprache, ihr unbegriffliches Ausdrucksmoment, das die Darstellung objektiviert, für das geschriebene Wort nutzbar zu machen. Als Über- und Umformung bisheriger sprachlicher Ausdrucksformen, in Auflösung vorgegebener Bedeutungszusammenhänge und Formen des Zusammenhangs von Worten soll die Darstellung die Bedeutungsvielfalt einzelner Sprachelemente ausspielen und dergestalt Begriffe zum Sprechen bringen, um die "Sprache der Dinge" (Adorno 1973, S. 96) nachzuahmen und auf diese Weise den, Schöpfungsakt' nachzuahmen, in dem Begriffe ihre Bedeutung erlangt haben. (Adorno 1974, S. 199)

Darstellung ist der Ausdruck einer neuen Zusammenstellung von Begriffen zum Zwecke ihrer Freisetzung aus festgefügten Bedeutungszusammenhängen; als Nichtidentität von Begriff und Erfahrung soll die Differenz zwischen Sache und Ausdruck in der Darstellung nicht zur Ruhe kommen und zu immer neueren Konstellationen herausfordern. In der "Ästhetischen Theorie" behauptet Adorno vom Ausdruck, dass er "der Widerpart des etwas Ausdrückens" ist, da sich sein "Sprachcharakter" von der "kommunikativen Sprache" unterscheidet, und zwar durch seinen "mimetischen Vollzug" von Sprache. (Adorno 1973, S. 171)

Mit diesem Hinweis haben wir eine weitere Antwort auf die eingangs gestellte Frage, warum Adorno die Kommunizierbarkeit eines jeden Gedankens als eine Fiktion bezeichnet. Denn inwieweit die Darstellung, die das Gedachte kommunizierbar, d. h. mitteilbar machen will, die Differenz von Ausdruck und Sache überhaupt unterläuft, macht Adorno abhängig von der Rückgewinnung und der Teilhabe am geschehnishaften Vollzug der Sprache, die die ‚gesprochene Sprache' insofern verliert, als sie in Form von Bedeutungszusammenhängen, Satzstrukturen und Sinnkontexten erfolgt. Dass die Begriffe bzw. Worte, indem sie ein Eigenleben entfalten, etwas von dem zurückerhalten würden, was sie während ihrer Bildung einmal hatten, ist eine ambivalente Behauptung. Denn konträr ist der Ausdruck dem Begriff nicht aus dem Grund, weil er sich vom Vollzug der Sprache noch nicht gelöst hat; vielmehr verwandelt der Ausdruck als ein solcher Vollzug den Begriff in das zurück, was sich in ihm chiffriert, und zwar mit Hilfe des Torsohaften, Polyvalenten und Vieldeutigen, das die Signifikanz ‚kommunikativer' Sprache aufbricht und dergestalt ‚unkommunizierbar', genauer gesagt: teilweise unkommunizierbar werden lässt. Denn die mimetisch künstlerische Sprachlichkeit stellt sich weniger in der völligen Negation der tradierten Sprachlichkeit her, eher durch die schrittweise Abweichung von gewohnten Zusammenhängen, bei der der "Konflikt von Ausdruck und Bedeutung in der Sprache […] nicht […] schlicht zugunsten des Ausdrucks entschieden", sondern "als Antinomie respektiert" wird. (Adorno 1974, S. 441)

Somit lässt sich als sprachliche Form der Ausdruck zunächst nur negativ, d. h. in seiner Differenz zur gebräuchlichen "Wortsprache" charakterisieren (Adorno 1976, S. 121), schließt er doch die Destruktion des Sinns des Dargestellten, d. h. den Bruch mit einer je schon vorgegebenen Vorstellung von der

Form und des Sinns am Dargestellten ein, durch die die Darstellung Transzendenz erlangen soll. (Adorno 1976, S. 39 f.) Dieses Verfahren lässt Gedanken nicht unkommunizierbar werden. Wie moderne Kunst findet auch die schriftstellerische Darstellung Gehör, aber kein Verständnis, weil sie ihre Sprache nicht an andere richtet, sondern die Form als etwas setzt, dem ihr (geläufiger) Gehalt zu widersprechen scheint. Wie überzeugend es auch klingen mag, wenn Adorno darauf verweist, dass die Paradoxie und Widersprüchlichkeit der Form die Möglichkeit einer Dechiffrierung der Begriffe bezeugt, so stellen sich doch ernsthafte Schwierigkeiten ein, wenn man berücksichtigt, dass der Ausdruck der Darstellung nur dann spricht, wenn das, was er mitzuteilen beabsichtigt, gehört und erhört wird.

Damit wären wir erneut bei unserer Ausgangsfrage: Gibt es Gedanken, die unkommunizierbar sind? In der Tat scheint es für Adorno unmitteilbare Gedanken zu geben, jedenfalls in dem Sinne, dass es nicht in die Macht des Autors liegt, seine Gedanken anderen in überzeugender Weise nahe zu bringen. Als Vollzugsform des Zusammenspiels von Rhetorik, Ausdruck, Sprache und Konstellation überbrückt die Darstellung diese Verlegenheit laut Adorno insofern, als das "Überredende der Kommunikation [...] (die) Bestimmung der Darstellung an sich" ist. Die Überredung ist abhängig von dem "Bezwingenden" der Konstruktion der Darstellung, die nicht die Sache abbilden sondern aus ihrem begrifflichen membra disiecta wiederherstellen möchte". (Adorno 1974, S. 31)

Eine solche Formulierung ruft jene Kritiken in Erinnerung, die die Definition der Rhetorik als eine Kunst der Überredung in der Weise deuten, dass der Zuhörer, überwältigt vom Redefluss des Redners und geblendet von der einleuchtenden Darlegung, nicht zur klaren Besinnung über das Gesagte kommt. Es scheint, als ob Adorno sich diesem Verständnis annimmt, wenn er nahe legt, dass die Darstellung dem Leser und Interpreten überreden soll, um diesen am Vollzug von Sprache teilhaben zu lassen, von dem er sich durch die Abkehr der Darstellung von der ‚kommunikativen' Sprache und der sprachlichen, hermetischen Introvertiertheit der Darstellung ausgesperrt fühlt. In Adornos Erörterung hat die nie endgültig abgeschlossene Anstrengung der Rhetorik, etwas glaubhaft zu machen, ihren Ursprung weniger in der bloßen Überredung als im Dilemma, die ‚kommunikative' Sprache aufgeben zu wollen, ohne ganz auf sie verzichten zu können. Adorno greift die tradierte Vorstellung von Rhetorik auf, jedoch in einer Weise, dass die Rhetorik in ihrer scheinbaren Schwäche ihre eigentliche Stärke demonstriert: Der Vorwurf, die Praxis der wohlgeformten Worte und der Kunst des sprachlichen Vortrages, die der Überredung oder Überzeugung der über den dargelegten Sachverhalt urteilenden Zuhörer dient, dürfte kaum etwas mit der Frage nach der Wahrheit zu tun haben, bietet Adorno ein methodisches Mittel, um scheinbar gültige Wahrheiten einer Welt der allgegenwärtigen instrumentellen Vernunft in Frage zu stellen.

Das ist jedoch lediglich der ideologiekritische Aspekt in Adornos Reaktualisierung der Rhetorik, deren systematischer Zusammenhang komplexer ist: Adornos Rückgriff auf die Rhetorik setzt keine wählbare Alternative zu einer Einsicht voraus, die man auch haben könnte, sondern zu der Plausibilität, die man nicht hat. In diesem Sinne ist m. E. Adornos Rede von den unkommunizierbaren Gedanken letztlich zu verstehen. Die Wiedererlangung der Vieldeutigkeit der Worte, deren Verschiedenheit nicht ganz verschieden ist, sondern an eine "Einheit des Wortes [...] in der Sachen" mahnen (Adorno 1974, S. 31), und die Durchbrechung des begrifflichen Identifikationsprinzips können mittels der Darstellung einleuchten, sind jedoch nicht beweisbar. Es gibt Gedanken, wie das Nichtidentische, über das sich nicht wie über andere Dinge verständigt werden kann, weil der Bezug "zu dem Gegenstand [...] auf die volle Durchsichtigkeit seiner logischen Genesis verzichtet", soll nicht der einzelne Gegenstand in der Form des Allgemeinen und Beständigen unvollständig zum Ausdruck kommen. Darin liegt eine tiefe "Unzulänglichkeit" (Adorno 1973, S. 100 f.), die der Hilfe der rhetorischen Überredungskunst nicht entbehren kann, deren Gleichsetzung mit einem Erzwingen zu dem tradierten Vorurteil der Rhetorik gehört, da die Zustimmung allein als das auf Widerruf erlangte Resultat der Überredung zu betrachten ist.

Wenn jedoch der tiefere Beweggrund des Überredens laut Kant im Fürwahrhalten zu suchen ist (Kant 1990, B 848, S. 687), das den Autor bewegt, seinen Lesern seine Auffassungen dergestalt mitzuteilen, dass sie von ihnen auch dann als einleuchtend anerkannt werden können, wenn sie nicht im Detail erläuterbar sind, schließt Adornos Prämisse, dass "die Schlüsselposition des Subjekts in der Erkenntnis [...] (die) Erfahrung" ist (Adorno 1977, S. 752), im Kontext der von ihm reaktualisierten Rhetorik eine Erfahrung ein, die sich als das beschreiben lässt, was der junge Hegel am Beispiel des erlebten Ereignisses der Taufe schildert: dass das Subjekt aus der Selbstverständlichkeit eines gewohnten Sprachhorizonts in andere Horizonte eintaucht und sich dabei so verändert, dass es in ein Andersgewordenes zurückkehrt. Die rhetorische Technik der Verwandlung der Sprache in eine assoziative 'Reihung', deren Elemente anders sich verknüpfen als in Subsumtion unter Vorgegebenes und

Bekanntes, korrigiert den Schein, dass das Subjekt sich jenseits von der Sprache ein Bild von der Welt macht. Denn es macht die nach geeigneten Worten vergebens suchende Erfahrung, dass es im Wandel der Sprache – durch die es erst zum Subjekt wird (Adorno 1974, S. 477) – sich selbst wandelt. In diesem Sinne betont Adorno, dass der "Denkende [...] sich zum Schauplatz" einer geistigen "Erfahrung" macht (Adorno 1974, S. 21), über die sprachlich sich Rechenschaft zu geben "Lücken" hinterlässt: Lücken – so der Titel des von mir erörterten Abschnitts der "Minima Moralia" –, die nicht subjektive Inkonsistenzen des Denkens verschulden, sondern sich daraus ergeben, dass sich das in der Sprache ausdrückende Subjekt "eine Relevanz vortäuscht, die ihm entzogen" ist (Adorno 1973, S. 178), da es, "hinter seiner Verdinglichung hertappend", durch das "mimetische Rudiment" einschränkt, was an "Sprache gewinnt". (Adorno 1973, S. 179) Mit dieser Äußerung aus der "Ästhetischen Theorie" verlegt Adorno nicht nur den Schwerpunkt von der Entgegensetzung von Wort und Auszudrückendem auf die Persistenz der im sprachlichen Ausdruck objektivierten Erfahrung; es entsteht auch der Eindruck, dass Adorno letztlich weder den Glauben an die welterschließende Kraft der Sprache noch an die Möglichkeit eines kognitiven Zugangs zur 'Sprache der Dinge' aufzugeben vermocht hat, in deren Möglichkeit ihn, wenn nicht Hegel, so doch die Einsicht skeptisch gestimmt haben muss, dass Sprache und Denken an die synthetische Form des Begriffs gebunden ist. (Adorno 1974, S. 471; vgl. Wischke 2005a, 2005b)

Literaturverzeichnis

Adorno, Theodor W. und Horkheimer, Max (1987): Dialektik der Aufklärung. In: Max Horkheimer, Gesammelte Schriften, Bd. 5, Frankfurt/M.
Adorno, Theodor W. (1989): Minima Moralia, Frankfurt/M.
Ders. (1982), Negative Dialektik, Frankfurt/M.
Ders. (1990), Zur Metakritik der Erkenntnistheorie, Frankfurt/M.
Ders. (1977), Stichworte: Dialektische Epilegomena, Abschnitt: Zu Subjekt und Objekt. In: Gesammelte Schriften, Bd. 10.2, Frankfurt/M.
Ders. (1973), Ästhetische Theorie, Frankfurt/M.
Ders. (1974), Noten zur Literatur, Frankfurt/M.
Ders. (1976), Philosophie der neuen Musik, Frankfurt/M.
Englisch, Felicitas (1990): Adorno und Hegel. Ein Missverständnis über die Sprache. In: F. Hager und H. Pfütze (Hg.), Das unerhört Moderne. Berliner Adorno-Tagung, Lüneburg, S. 28-47.
Gadamer, Hans-Georg (1999): Hegel und Heidegger (1971), Gesammelte Werke, Tübingen, Bd. 3, S. 87-101.
Ders. (2000), Hermeneutische Entwürfe: Vorträge und Aufsätze, Tübingen.

Hegel, Georg Friedrich Wilhelm (1973): Phänomenologie des Geistes, Werkausgabe, Redaktion E. Moldenhauer und K. M. Michel, Frankfurt/M., Bd. 3.

Kant, Immanuel (1961): Vorlesung über Encyclopädie und Logik, Berlin.

Ders. (1990), Kritik der reinen Vernunft, Werkausgabe, Bd. III, hrsg. von Wilhelm Weischedel, Frankfurt/M.

Kopperschmidt, Josef (1994): Nietzsches Entdeckung der Rhetorik. Rhetorik im Dienste der unreinen Vernunft, in: Josef Kopperschmidt u. a. Hrsg.), Nietzsche oder "Die Sprache ist Rhetorik", München, S. 39-62.

Müller-Lauter, Wolfgang (1999): Über Werden und Wille zur Macht. Nietzsche Interpretationen I, Berlin New York.

Nietzsche, Friedrich (1988a): Nachlass 1885-1887, Kritische Studienausgabe, hrsg. v. G. Colli und M. Montinari, Bd. 12, München.

Ders. (1988b), Über Wahrheit und Lüge im außermoralischen Sinne, Kritische Studienausgabe, hrsg. v. G. Colli und M. Montinari, München, Bd. 1, S. 875-890.

Scholze, Britta (2000): Kunst als Kritik. Adornos Weg aus der Dialektik, Würzburg.

Wischke, Mirko (2005a): Die Schwäche der Schrift. Adorno über Sprache und die Fiktion der vollständigen Darlegung von Gedanken. In: Blickwechsel. XI. Lateinamerikanischer Germanistenkongress (ALEG), Akten: Band 2, Sao Paulo, S. 300-305.

Ders. (2005b), Ungleiches gleich zu machen. Über den Zusammenhang von Tausch und Sprache bei Adorno. In: Georg Mein & Franziska Schössler (Hg.), Tauschprozesse, Transcript. Verlag für Kommunikation, Kultur und soziale Praxis, Bielefeld, S. 107-129.

CULTURAL RIGHTS AND LIBERAL MULTICULTURALISM[1]

MORTEN EBBE JUUL NIELSEN

Department of Philosophy and Science Studies
Roskilde University Center

The question of multiculturalism and cultural rights looms large in contemporary political philosophical debate, and rightly so: these are some of the most pertinent questions facing modern liberal democracies. I this article, I present and discuss a series of theories about how liberal theory should face up to the challenge of multiculturalism, or "the fact of pluralism." It is argued that two extremes in the debate, communitarianism and liberal neutrality, are both inadequate responses to the challenge of multiculturalism, and that liberal theory ought to steer a middle course between those. That middle course is expressed in a focus on liberal citizenship: liberal theory should neither value culture qua culture (the communitarian or "identity-politics" point of view, nor should it ignore culture (the liberal neutralist point of view.)

Do minorities have cultural rights, i.e., rights against other persons that protect and further culture? Do majorities? If so, what kind of right? And how does liberal political philosophy and the idea of cultural rights fit together, if at all?

These are some of the questions regarding cultural rights addressed in this paper. They are important questions in their own right. Furthermore, whereas the question of cultural rights was probably easy to subsume under some more general heading in earlier days, the question becomes ever more pertinent in societies that labour under what Rawls called "the fact of pluralism", or what a host of other writers have called *multiculturalism*: the existence of a plurality of possibly mutually exclusive or even hostile encompassing ways of life within the same polity.

Cultural rights are commonly regarded as group rights. However, some liberal philosophers, uneasy to differing degrees about the cogency of positing anything beyond individuals as proper right-holders, have also endorsed cultural rights on a purely individualist basis.

Common to the way most philosophers talk about cultural rights is that they are at the very least connected somehow to the existence of relatively stable and easily identifiable collective and encompassing ways of life, typically with reference to linguistic or nationalistic identities (like the French-Canadians or the Basques), ethnicity (like the Pakistani in Great Britain), or religion (like Mormons or Muslims.)

The arguments I will try to unfold here take as background a familiar fissure dividing liberals and anti-liberals concerning multiculturalism: One liberal attitude concerning multiculturalism and its correlates (identity, recognition, and so forth) is to deny the relevance of (group) identity and culture from the political point of view. Whereas such matters might be of prime importance to individuals, the right liberal standpoint is to ignore them, to adopt a "politics of indifference." In a well-known phrase: the state ought to be *neutral* vis-à-vis the more comprehensive, substantial goals and conceptions of the good held true by citizens.

The standard reply, made by communitarians and others who wish to adopt a "politics of recognition" is that liberal neutrality is either unfeasible or undesirable. In effect, a neutral political programme will mean that the culture, identity, and the comprehensive goals of the majority will be recognised and supported over and before the culture, identity, and goals of minorities. The whole point of multiculturalism – at least, if we abstract from the mundane world of political struggle for particular interests – is that only by acknowledging the marginalised and vulnerable position of out-of-mainstream cultures can we pay the proper respect to the individuals who "belong" outside the mainstream ethnic, religious, sexual etc. culture. Overlooking their vulnerability is a way of treating minorities as less than equals; hence, liberal neutrality is a sham.

I will argue that none of these standpoints are adequate. Politics of indifference or *neutrality* is not the right way to deal with the issues at hand. Moreover, other liberal attempts to reconcile traditional liberal concerns (for freedom, respect for the individual etc.) with certain forms of quasi-collective rights (Kymlicka, 1989 and 1995) falter as well. Against communitarians and other adherents of politics of recognition, and with the standard liberal position, I will argue that the illiberal consequences of a politics of recognition or identity are dire indeed.

The way to deal with the issues at hand is not a communitarian (or a liberal, for that sake) politics of recognition, nor is it a liberal neutralist politics of indifference or neutrality. Rather, we should concentrate on developing a theory of liberal *citizenship* that ignores neither the fact that culture largely determines both the prospects and values of individuals and the stability of a liberal political regime (hence, we should never ignore culture, and we ought not to be neutral regarding culture) nor the facts that individual wellbeing is what ultimately matters (hence, we have no reasons to respect culture *per se*) and that cultures are not necessarily just or liberal.

The paper, then, falls in three sections: the first section will mainly deal with matters of definition and some technical points regarding rights, multiculturalism, and liberalism. The second will deal with cultural rights. The third, and very short section, will deal with liberal multiculturalism and liberal citizenship.

Setting the Stage: Rights

I want to frame the basic question of multiculturalism in terms of rights. Note that the following does not rely on holding rights to have a fundamental status; rather, I find it pragmatically convenient to take recourse to a rights-framework for the problem at hand. Hence, the basic question is whether we owe minorities (or majorities, for that sake) cultural rights beyond those rights normally implied by plausible political platforms.

Furthermore, I assume that the discussion is most interesting if one adopts a *liberal* framework. Embracing communitarian premises makes the argument for cultural rights rather less interesting, as it makes any argument to the effect that groups have rights superfluous (I take it to be a defining feature of communitarianism that groups, whether they be nations, tribes, religions, etc. have intrinsic moral importance *qua* groups.)

I wish to adopt as innocent and uncontroversial a definition of rights as possible. Hence:

Df1.: *Rights*: The existence of a right means that someone has an interest that is (best) furthered by holding that right; and rights impose duties.

Both legs of this definition are important: first of all, one should note that rights are necessarily connected to interests (but note that the definition is open to radically different interpretations of "interests")

The "rights impose duties" part is equally important. It circumscribes the range of rights in a way I believe most will agree is reasonable. In principle, there are no limitations to the kind and amount of interests I can have. I could have an interest in having my own, live unicorn, for instance. However, most will agree that I do not *eo ipso* have a right to a unicorn, i.e., there are no other people that have a duty to provide me with a unicorn. Naturally, the limitation implicit in the "rights impose duties" part of the definition go much further than this. At least two different ideas or principles contribute to this limitation:

Df.: *The "no grossly burdensome duties" proviso*: Rights impose only duties that are not grossly burdensome.

In general, there is consensus that there is a limit to the kind of duties we owe each other. Again, different philosophers will come to different conclusions about those limits, and their justification. Some consequentialists will argue that we have an individual duty to promote welfare, up to the point where doing so begins to diminish overall welfare. This might mean that I have a duty to sacrifice my life to bring about a state of affairs in which a large number of people have their preference for ice cream satisfied. True, the beneficiaries of my sacrifice ought to lament the fact that I had to die in order to bring about the said state of affairs; but suppose it is a *really* good ice cream and a *lot* of people *really* wanted to have the ice cream. Conversely, some deontologists will argue that I do not have a duty to promote welfare, that deontological constraints impose limits to the kind of duties I owe others. So even though I by sacrificing, say, half a pint of my blood that happens to contain special anti-vira, could cure millions of people of a debilitating disease, I am under no special duty to do so.

But surely, none of these extreme standpoints really gets it right about what "grossly burdensome" implies. This is not the place to settle this question; yet, I take it for granted that justifiable duties go further than implied by my straw deontologist and are less burdensome than implied by my straw consequentialist.

It seems natural to believe that this proviso takes on a special significance when applied to political (collective) rather than individual affairs. Political decisions are decisions on behalf of many people. The law covers all agents in a polity. Individual decisions might affect many people, but normally affect the agent in question before and more than others. I might choose to give up my life in order to bring about a state of affairs in which a multitude get some very good ice cream; it seems a lot harder to claim that my fellow citizens are under an obligation to do so if they could, etc. In a phrase, there are limits to what we can reasonably demand of each other; to the burdens we can legitimately impose on fellow citizens. This might be a purely instrumental consideration. We cannot expect a law demanding huge sacrifices to be effective, and it might undermine other, more modest and reasonable claims of the law. Or it might have roots in deeper considerations about autonomy, the separateness of persons etc. Be that as it may, there seems to be widespread consensus on at least the practical rule of thumb that the sacrifices imposed on our fellow citizens ought to be somewhat less burdensome than those we expect from a perfect moral altruist. Hence, the "no grossly burdensome duties" is especially pertinent when applied to political decisions.

Df.: *The "only legitimate interests" proviso:* Only legitimate interests can ground duties.

This is another potentially controversial theme. Two discussions are relevant: 1) are all interests directly person-affecting, and 2) for the person-affecting interests, how, if at all, are they limited?

Regarding 1) some will claim that the scope of relevant interests is exhausted by those that are directly person-affecting: hence, other considerations, like a just distribution of goods or wellbeing, the existence of a virtuous or a thriving culture, etc., are exhausted when their impact on individuals is exhausted. I might have a legitimate interest in a just distribution of goods only to the extent it serves mine or some other person's well-being, all things considered. There are no further interests to be taken into consideration. Some disagree. Again, I will not try to settle that question here; only note that that both positions could agree on the proviso as it stands.

Regarding 2) most will agree that there are kinds of interests that, even though they are in at least one sense genuine (i.e., in the sense that some relevant agent actually have, or perceives to have, one of those interest), they are not genuinely legitimate interests. The would-be rapist might have an overwhelming urge to molest a small child, yet, we do not perceive this to be a legitimate interest.

Taking for granted that any reasonable conception of "rights" must confirm the provisos stated, let us proceed to the question of multiculturalism.

Multiculturalism

When we use the term "multiculturalism", we refer to either of two general meanings: we can either use it to denote a state of affairs; the existence of two or more relatively distinct cultures within the same polity, or, it specifies a moral idea or ideal about how to deal with the empirical situation just sketched.

I have only little to say about the first. I take it to be the case that nearly all polities today are in fact multicultural, at least to some degree. I shall use the phrase "sociological multiculturalism" to refer to this fact of multiculturalism.

The second use denotes various moral replies or stances towards sociological multiculturalism; replies that to various degrees embrace sociological multiculturalism as a positive (i.e., good) fact, or at least one that we should not necessarily see as an undesirable feature of modern life.[2] I will refer to this broad category as "moral multiculturalism."

Clearly, the two different senses are related. But I find it necessary to keep them apart. In the political discourse one often finds arguments that conflate the two senses, as in "multiculturalism is a [sociological] fact; therefore, we ought to embrace [moral] multiculturalism", which is clearly a *non sequitur*.

I shall distinguish between two different senses of moral multiculturalism:

1) Df.: *Liberal multiculturalism*: Multiculturalism is not only a sociological fact; it is also at least possible that we need to acknowledge that different citizens of the same political order belong to different cultures, and hence, face different challenges in order to fulfil standard liberal aspirations towards equality and liberty. The relevant standard for evaluating the need for acknowledgment of cultural differences is *political*; it originates (predominantly, at least) from the liberal political ideas irrespective of their rooting in different cultures.

2) Df.: *Communitarian multiculturalism*: Multiculturalism is not only a sociological fact; it is also the case that we need to acknowledge that different citizens of the same political order belong to different cultures, and hence, they have different needs of recognition from the state. The relevant standard(s) for judging the need of recognition is *cultural*; it originates (predominantly, at least) from the ideas imbedded in the different cultures of the polity.

Another way of bringing out the difference between these families of conceptualisation: Liberal multiculturalism assigns at most *instrumental* and contingent value to the values of particular cultures *qua* cultures, whereas communitarians can assign *intrinsic* value to the values of cultures *qua* cultures.

These ways of defining the positions are probably somewhat unusual. I by no means intend that these are the only positions available, logically or conceptually. They are meant as opposite ends of a rather small portion of a much longer spectrum of theories. However, I believe that most of the interesting discussion takes place in this section of the spectrum.

II. Liberalism and Cultural Rights

There is something particularly interesting and somewhat puzzling about the connection between liberalism and culture in general, and liberalism and multiculturalism in particular. One natural first response is that liberalism *per se* has no problem with (sociological) multiculturalism: that the very point of liberalism is tolerance (and perhaps diversity); hence, liberalism is the one major kind of political ideology that has the *least* trouble with accommodating the fact of cultural pluralism (cf.: Kukathas (1998), p. 690). This immediate response is not entirely off track: liberalism, when compared with certain conservative, theocratic, or republican ideologies, *is* more accommodating to differences and pluralism; at least, liberalism is not married to some monocultural conception of value tied to the history of the nation or some other factor that is viewed as irrelevant from the liberal, moral point of view.

On the other hand, it might seem that, on that very account, liberals cannot *care* for culture: the price for liberal tolerance and its elevated status as free from allegiances to a specific cultural background is that a liberal regime cannot undertake to support or suppress culture(s.) All it can do is to maintain certain rules and rights for citizens; rules and rights that are seen, often *per credo*, as independent from specific cultural settings. *Mutatis mutandi*, this is the view of standard liberal neutralists like Rawls (1971; 1993), Dworkin (1983; 1995), Larmore (1987) and Ackerman (1980).[3]

Against this, I maintain that liberals *must* take culture into consideration, both in making theory and politics:

(1) The first type of argument to the effect that liberals must care about culture asserts that cultural rights have their proper ground in considerations of distributional justice. Liberals, especially those of a non-libertarian persuasion, ought to be concerned with equality in terms that go beyond mere formal equality of legal rights etc., i.e., with equality of resources or welfare, or opportunity for welfare, etc.

How does culture and cultural rights enter this picture? Liberals can view the question of cultural membership as a question of *distributional justice* (see, e.g., Kymlicka (1989), p. 162.) Cultural membership or background is part of the allocation of goods; hence, you can have "more" or "less" relative to some standard, e.g., the average citizen. A member of a minority will then, *ceteris paribus*, tend to have less (or at least less spending potential due to higher costs) than the member of the majority. Liberal egalitarians can then advocate an argument for cultural (minority) rights along the following lines: barring special circumstances, people ought to be treated equally in the distribution of goods and burdens. But members of minorities will have a relatively smaller proportion of "cultural goods" – e.g., they will have to spend relatively more of their allocated resources to maintain their preferred cultural way of life than members of the majority culture. Accordingly, to obtain liberal equality we ought to redistribute means or legal rights, directly or indirectly, in favour of minorities (I shall return to Kymlicka's defence of cultural rights below.)

Defences of this sort draw much of their intuitive appeal from the same sources as Rawls and Dworkin when they appeal to considerations of fairness in the social and natural lotteries: our distributional fate (whether we think of this in terms of resources or welfare) ought not to depend on factors that are "arbitrary from the moral point of view"; the cultural circumstances in which we are born and hence, the preferences and values we have are, at least to some extent,[4] arbitrary and beyond our immediate control and responsibility; thus, we have a right not to be treated unequally because of our cultural circumstances.

(2) The second kind of argument contends that cultural rights are necessary for the survival of a liberal regime itself. Let us suppose that liberalism involves autonomy in the sense that qualified individual freedom is among the prime goals for a liberal society. Several further claims now follow: there must be an adequate range of valuable options from which an agent can choose; a certain level of education and cultural advancement; adequate and sufficiently reliable

and rich sources of information; relatively generous physical circumstances; some amount of personal liberty; political freedom, the rule of law, and general tolerance (see Raz (1986), pp. 307ff, 369ff).

In sum, because it consists mainly of liberal individuals, a liberal society/state cannot be indifferent as regards the *content* of its own cultural setting. Liberal freedom is a historical achievement, not something that falls to us like manna from heaven, and it can only be maintained within certain cultural conditions.

But why should a liberal society consist of liberal individuals? Perhaps this is too strong a formulation, but it seems plausible to suggest that citizens in a liberal state must endorse some liberal values – e.g. individual freedom and some form of commitment to equality – if the liberal project is to succeed. At the very least, such citizens should not be openly hostile to the liberal project.

Taken together these claims imply that the institutions and the options available in a liberal society must be *of a certain kind* – they must protect, sustain, and further liberal culture. Common sense tells us that a society without universal basic education, a rich variety of arts and literature, and a certain amount of vivacity in the "marketplace of ideas", hardly qualifies as a liberal society at all. Either that, or it will be a liberal society only for a very short period.

Historically, liberals have been concerned about the possibly excessive power of the state precisely because they regarded education, art and so on as institutions that are too important and too fragile for the state to handle. But acknowledging the importance and fragility of these institutions shows that a liberal state cannot consistently remain completely aloof vis-à-vis the cultural setting. Its ongoing existence depends on a liberal society or culture, and the claim that the liberal state should not care about the existence of the liberal state displays a certain internal tension, to say the least.

If we want to implement (or encourage or secure) rights or institutions that are valuable, we are also required to implement (or encourage or secure) the conditions that are required for these rights or institutions to flourish. If we want the end (a liberal state etc.) we are rationally committed to willing the requisite means. So, it seems that liberals must be concerned about the cultural setting after all.[5]

(3) A third argument to the effect that liberals cannot ignore the cultural setting asserts that doing so will allow injustices in the personal sphere – injustices that cannot be overlooked by any just regime. Different versions of this argu-

ment has been put forward by Cohen (Cohen (1997), see especially pp. 15ff) and Okin (see e.g., Okin (1989) chap. 5). To be exact, these writers claim that liberalism cannot ignore *the private sphere*: a traditional liberal idea (or bias) is that principles of justice, and to a large extent, the reach of law, are applicable to *public* matters alone (see also Edmundson, especially part III). The critique against this is that injustices, distributional or otherwise, are as likely in the private as they are in the public sphere; hence, the traditional liberal myopia where private matters are bracketed off the political agenda is incoherent and unattractive.

This readily transforms itself into the argument that liberals ought not to ignore the cultural sphere as such. Okin stresses (as does Rawls) that the family is a "school of justice". To a large extent, we adopt preferences and behavioural patterns from our families, but families in themselves are patterned after culturally imbedded traditions and conceptions. Moreover, cultural traditions naturally influence individuals in the same way as does families, and if the family can be an arena of injustice (which is obviously the case), so can the culture (for a related argument that goes more directly to the point of the suppressive potential in culture, see Danley (1991), pp. 171ff).

Three Liberal Conceptions of Cultural Rights

Beside the fact that liberal political philosophy and practice cannot ignore culture, what bearings do the arguments of the previous section have on the question of liberalism and multiculturalism? To see this I will use Okin's critique of three different liberal attempts to fuse cultural rights and liberalism (for the following, see Okin (1998), pp. 667ff). I will concentrate mainly on Halbertal and Margalit's defence of strong positive rights of assistance for cultural minorities in a liberal state; not because I believe this is the *best* attempt, but because it brings out several important issues about multiculturalism. Furthermore, it allows me to launch some sceptical arguments that I believe have not been adequately dealt with by defenders of (moral) multiculturalism.

Identity and Cultural Rights

One attempt to ground cultural rights within a liberal political framework is made by Halbertal and Margalit (Halbertal/Margalit (1994). The key claims of their article are that

> Human beings have a right to culture – not just any culture, but their own.[6]

and

> ... the individual's right to culture stems from the fact that every person has an *overriding* interest in his personal identity – that is, in preserving his way of life and the traits that are central identity components for him and the other members of his cultural group.[7]

In fact, this overriding interest is even stronger than traditional liberal concerns for freedom; even if cultures "... flout the rights of the individual in a liberal society" (H/M, p. 491, cf.: Okin (1998), p. 671). This becomes even clearer: "In our view, which links the right to culture with identity *rather than freedom*." (H/M, p. 506.)

The upshot of Halbertal and Margalit's idea of cultural rights is that even extraordinarily illiberal cultures should not only be left alone; they have a right to assistance that makes it able for them to flourish; otherwise, we might violate individuals' "right to belonging" – if a given culture ceases to exist, one cannot choose to belong to that culture (H/M, p. 506ff).

So, Halbertal and Margalit's defence of cultural rights departs from traditional liberal philosophy in at least three ways: First, even though it is certainly possible to read the defence as being in accordance with the standard liberal assumption of moral individualism (i.e., the idea that, no matter what the metaphysical status of the individual is, the individual is the only thing that matters intrinsically, morally speaking), the community (the culture) is certainly conceived of as considerably more important than is the norm in liberal political thought. The community takes on a moral life of its own, insofar the *overriding* interest of individuals lies in their identity, and that identity is simply defined in terms of the community.

Secondly, not only is identity given a prominent overriding role, it even overrides *freedom*: the right to identity is "basic and primary" (H/M, p. 506) and for individuals whose identities are bound up with illiberal cultures, "... the ability to choose has little if any value ..." This links the Halbertal/Margalit defence of cultural rights with a communitarian rather than a liberal framework: the standards of the communities in question are the baselines, not the standards of the liberal political society.

Thirdly, Halbertal and Margalit depart from the standard liberal assumption of state neutrality. They claim that the state is "... obligated to abjure its neutrality... not for the sake of the good of the majority, but in order to make it possible for members of minority groups to retain their identity" (H/M, p. 492).

Two Major Problems Concerning Cultural Rights

There are, I believe, insurmountable problems with this defence of cultural rights. I will concentrate on just two major problems, one is about the moral implications of this line of thought, another is about the premise that we have an overriding interest in identity. The arguments to follow are *not* purely *ad hominem*; I believe they apply quite generally to the multiculturalism controversy.

First and foremost, I see no way in which it is even superficially plausible that a *liberal* state should impose burdens on their citizens in order to, not only protect, but actually sustain and further illiberal subcultures within society. The question to ask is: do we harm someone if we do not support the culture of his or hers' choice? (Okin (1998), p.672.) Only if the following hold true: that non-support will mean that the culture in question fades away in the absence of support, and that alternative culture(s) available are, in fact, somehow worse for those individuals who would favour the potentially disappearing culture.[8]

The first question – will the culture disappear if it is not supported – is of course predominantly an empirical matter. But note that many religious and national minority cultures seem to survive even when they do not get financial or other kinds of positive support from the state, or get only little.

A more philosophically interesting question is whether a culture that cannot "stand on its own" really is a culture worthy of much care. This is of course relative to the circumstances: no morally good culture has much chance of survival in a despotic tyranny. But let us suppose the political framework in which a culture exists is a fairly liberal one, and that individuals in this framework are reasonably well educated, are reasonably rational, are reasonably free of irrational bias, and have an adequately wide range of (cultural) options from which to choose. Suppose furthermore that there is a reasonably just, or not downright unjust, distribution of goods.[9] In what sense is a culture that cannot exist in the absence of further public support under these conditions a culture worth caring for? *Ex hypothesi*, citizens do not choose to spend their resources to support it; hence, it becomes unclear *for whom* it is we should keep that culture alive. And it is even less clear whether or not the means used for its support are not better spent in support of some cultural option that people actually *do* wish to support.

The second question – are the alternatives worse for the individual who wishes to belong to a certain culture if that culture fades away – is of course relative to the alternatives. Do we *harm* that person if we do not assist an ailing culture? That can only be answered if we take the alternative cultures into consideration. But can we really say that we *always* harm a person by forcing him or her into adopting a new culture – passively, by letting the culture in question fade away by not supporting it, or actively, by interfering in the cultural marketplace? The answer is surely no. Halbertal and Margalits prime case story – which is one of the ultra-orthodox Jewish communities in Israel – is one such example. It is very hard to see a liberal justification for even accepting the existence of a culture that preaches deep and pervasive inequality between the sexes; denies anything but the most rudimentary education for its members; and perpetuates bizarre moralistic infringements on especially their own, but also on others' basic rights (see H/M, pp. 492ff, cf.: Okin (1998), pp. 671ff). How can it constitute *harm* to individuals that we do not support a culture that do harm to individuals? At the very least, is this not a discussion that must be approached in a piecemeal, case-by-case way rather than by some fixed principle which accords an overriding weight to peoples' identity rather than their well-being?

A Right to Belonging?

The idea that we have an overriding interest in identity is puzzling in several ways. If we do have such a right, why should we not conceive of it as a right to *choose* and *evaluate* different cultures? And perhaps to build and develop rather than a right to preserve different already existing cultures? Among other things, this would imply that the standards of education, public deliberation etc. cannot effortlessly be those of illiberal cultures themselves, but rather of a more genuinely liberal kind, emphasising freedom of information, certain standards of rationality, and equality between the sexes –standards that Halbertal and Margalit explicitly state that it should be allowed for minority cultures to flout (H/M, pp. 492f, 506ff, cf.: Okin (1998), pp. 671ff).

Furthermore, if we have an overriding right to belonging, why is this right confined to relatively well-defined cultures like the ultra-orthodox Jews which are at centre stage for Halbertal and Margalit? They define a culture as "a comprehensive way of life ... as the way of life of an encompassing group, such as an ethnic, religious, or national group ... A group of carpenters today is not in this category: a carpenters' guild in medieval times was perhaps such an encompassing group." (H/M, pp. 497f.) However, why should our "overriding interest" in identity be confined to such groups? Surely, there are other kinds of group-related identities that are every way as "encompassing" and defining of the person as ethnic, religious, or national groups. Think of fanatical Trekkies or deadheads,[10] nomading from convention to convention or concert gig to concert gig, living in their own circles regulated by their own special codes of conduct etc. Or imagine activist members of sexual minorities, whose political and personal values and horizons are defined by their sexuality. Is it anything but a romantic bias that we ascribe a deeper, more foundational status to identities that are linked to, e.g., religiously defined groups, than we do to the Ecologically Aware Gay Masochists of San Francisco?[11] In the end, who does not properly belong, in an identity-relevant way, to *some* culture that could plausibly be said to be a minority? And hence, we all deserve special, cultural rights on an equal footing. But if everyone belongs to a minority, there is no special need for minority rights – ordinary, individual rights will suffice.[12]

The Value of "Belonging"

Moreover, we need to consider more carefully what the conditions for a culture to be valuably "mine" are than Halbertal and Margalit do. Some things are valuable for me without being dependent on *my* contribution towards their existence, at least without my active, positive contribution towards them. An example is a relatively clean environment: living in a pollution-free environment is valuable for me, no matter whether I have done anything to secure it.

Other things are less valuable, or even worthless, if *I* have not exercised my capacities: winning a 100-yard dash is worthless if I only win because a freak blast of wind carried me faster towards the goal line than my opponents. Having a brain implant that allows me to play Bach's Goldberg variations exactly like Glenn Gould is worthless because it is not *my* efforts, *my* soul that is expressed in the interpretation. Sure, there might be great instrumental value in these pursuits (are they really pursuits in the classical sense of the word?). But intrinsic value is radically diminished, or even completely eradicated, in examples like these. We might call such activities for *achievement-sensitive*; only by actively engaging in their pursuit are they valuable (or, alternatively, their intrinsic value is relative to the active engagement of agents').

Now, it is a pertinent question whether the value of one's cultural identity is somehow achievement-sensitive. Is cultural belonging and cultural identity not a kind of *activity*, rather than a background condition like the existence of a relatively clean environment? And if so, is it an achievement-sensitive activity, wholly or partially?

I believe this is the case. Cultural belonging is a kind of activity because one does not simply belong to a culture in virtue of one's "bare existence": if I do not from time to time actively engage in pursuits that are at least partially shaped and flavoured by a culture, the sense in which I belong to that culture is extremely vague. And following Raz (see Raz (1986), pp. 307ff *et circa*), we might say that personal well-being consist, to a large degree, in the success of one's socially defined important pursuits.[13] I believe the same goes for the value of cultural belonging as such: *I* strive to develop as a philosopher, to *achieve* that identity in its special form, which implies more than mere parroting of the great philosophers of our culture.[14] Being hypnotized and subconsciously trained to repeat all the words of, say, Quine, is not succeeding in my important pursuits at all.

But if exercising autonomy is necessary for one's cultural belonging to be important, then we cannot ignore the fact that cultures are accommodating to the value of autonomous choice to very differing degrees: We cannot claim that cultural identity is valuable independently of the degree it is compatible with the value of autonomy. Cultural identity is achievement sensitive. But this means that we ought not respect persons' cultural identity in the abstract without evaluating and factoring in the degree to which different cultures make it possible for individuals to *achieve*, as opposed to merely *adopt*, their cultural identities.

Romantics, communitarians, and other kinds of cultural relativists will protest that the very idea that the value of cultural identity is achievement-sensitive is a liberal construction; that only autonomy-endorsing cultures ascribe such an elevated status to the idea of autonomy.

There are two flaws in that reply. First, notice that the claim that the state ought to accommodate a diversity of cultures is always made in the context of *liberal* states. However, liberal states are not free-floating entities; they are rooted in liberal cultures or societies. And the cultures to which a liberal state owes some special consideration is embedded in at least one very important *liberal* framework, that of the state and the law. Hence, even illiberal cultures (in a liberal state) are in at least one important aspect liberal.[15] Furthermore, neither men nor cultures are islands; members of illiberal cultures in liberal states are, as a matter of fact, exposed and influenced by their surrounding liberal cultures. It becomes a pertinent, albeit largely empirical, question, whether and to what degree individual members of illiberal cultures become "tainted" by the liberal values of their "host" culture.[16] The point is that if the romantic critic of autonomy wishes to argue that members of illiberal cultures in liberal states do not, or cannot, see the value of autonomy, then that line of critique might founder on the empirical fact that those individuals do in fact endorse liberal values such as autonomy,[17] or, that the minority culture in question would not exist in the absence of a liberal framework that allows different cultures to exist at all.

Second, it is arguable that, even if members of illiberal cultures deny the value of autonomy, and hence, that the value of cultural identity is achievement-sensitive, they are simply wrong.

Culture and Individual

Conservative Romantics tend to believe that the value of culture lies exactly in the *denial* of the view that culture is created and achieved. The culture, they might assert, is something larger than the individual whose qualitative horizons are simply embedded in, or copied from, the community. In this lies a thought that the culture provides values and *mores* that are "unquestionable"; they are, to twist a Rawlsian phrase, "self-authenticating sources of valid claims."[18] It is not that Romantics necessarily believe that cultures are immutable – although an air of platonic essentialism is surely detectable in many communitarian conceptions of culture – the point is rather that the community and its values transcend the individual, and thereby provide the agent with an "objective" source of values, traditions, standards etc.

In one sense, Romantics are right: the community (or communities) and culture (or cultures) one is born into *do* provide the individual with his or her values, traditions, and standards. Even the most reflective individual can only transcend the values of his or her upbringing by being exposed to *other* values and cultures *or* if the community and culture of his or her upbringing and formation in itself values reflectivity and critical thought.

But it is exactly in being right about this that the conservative romantics, or those who hold that one's cultural identity constitute an overriding interest, *no matter what the substantial content of the identity/culture*, are proven wrong. To see this, consider the following:

Either one's cultural identity is of overriding interest, no matter what the content of this is. *Ex hypothesi*, any culture is equal in the sense that it does not matter what culture one belongs to, as long as one belongs. This means that we have no independent reason to respect or protect or sustain cultures *qua* cultures: as long as we make sure that individuals do belong to *a*, but not *a specific* culture, we do not violate individuals' rights. This means that we could, gradually or radically, persuade or coerce individuals of minority cultures to adopt the majority culture. Sure, there will be transition-costs,[19] but these are easily justified when we bring future generations into the picture. For it is less costly to nourish one rather than two or several cultures.

Alternatively, one's cultural identity is of overriding interest, only on the condition that its content meets certain standards.[20] But this opens the door to *comparisons* between cultures, and, I venture, to comparisons about the *quality* of different cultures. Hence, we can not say that we respect persons' interest simply by letting them belong to *a* culture; rather, we ought to respect the plausible second-order interest we all have that we wish to belong to culture that actually serves our interests best. And, unless one assumes some far-fetched version of cultural relativism, in which it is argued that our true interests are simply *exhausted* by the standards of one's present cultural circumstances – implying, e.g. that the interests of a battered housewife in a patriarchal culture are best served by her continued submission – this implies that we do not necessarily respect persons by respecting their present cultural identity, but rather that we respect them by bringing about the state of affairs where they belong to a culture that serves their *true* interest.

If this sounds illiberally paternalistic, one might change focus slightly from the content of cultures to their ability to provide individuals with the capacity and opportunity to choose as freely as is possible between cultures. But that is more or less a statement of one of liberalism's core justifications: by supporting and respecting qualified, autonomous choice, we respect persons and promote wellbeing. And this again implies that, from a liberal point of view, we do not respect persons by ignoring their cultural conditions, and we have no reason to believe that our duties are fulfilled when we let the fate of individuals depend on arbitrary cultural circumstances. Quite the opposite: we should actively pursue politics that enable individuals to evaluate and criticise those circumstances, and this might very well mean that we have a duty to change illiberal cultures, rather than preserve them.

So, Halbertal and Margalit's suggestion that we have an overriding interest in our cultural identity does not yield the result they are after: strong cultural rights to assistance for just any culture. If we should ignore the contents of cultures, there are no reasons to believe that we should support one culture rather than another, for persons can come to belong to any culture. If we should not ignore the content, we should either pay attention to the specifics of relevant cultures and then we might plausibly come to the conclusion that we do not respect persons by respecting their present cultural belonging (because it does not serve their interests best), or we should simply be liberals, insisting that a culture, in order to qualify for protection, must provide the necessary background for qualified autonomous choice.

If we emphasise these dimensions of "a right to identity": that the right is a right to *choose* and *evaluate* different cultures, the focus is changed from cultures to individuals, which is surely more in keeping with the liberal point of view. Perhaps it is this liberal point of view which is actually the target of Halbertal and Margalits critique. But if that is the case, they should argue so clearly and explicitly, and not under a liberal cloak. Halbertal and Margalit do nothing to show that strong cultural rights are compatible with a liberal point of view.

The Right to be Left Alone

Halbertal and Margalit's line of thought eschews liberal neutrality. By supporting specific cultures, and taking their own, controversial conceptions of the good as basic, the state cannot remain neutral. But not all defenders of liberal cultural rights want to give up neutrality. One such defender is Kukathas. Kukathas believes that neutrality should be upheld (Kukathas (1992), p.108, (1998), pp. 690f, 696) and, indeed, the tenor of his argument is that liberalism *per se* cannot be squared with (positive) cultural rights or collective rights of any kind. Rather, cultures (to be more precise, individuals in cultures) have a right to be "left alone", i.e., they have a negative right against others that they do not meddle with their internal affairs, at least within certain limits.[21]

This obviously reflects some of what I discussed above as the third reason why liberals cannot ignore the cultural sphere. Traditionally – or by *fiat* – liberals want to leave people as free as is possible to live their lives as they see fit. Whatever is private is not the business of the state. Accordingly, Kukathas believes that if and to the extent people "acquiesce" to a culture and its standards, this legitimises liberal non-interference (Kukathas (1992), p. 121ff; cf.: Okin (1998), p. 674.) This conjoins (implicitly) with another theme from the traditional liberal arsenal, namely *consent*. If we consent to something, it is at least *prima facie* legitimate.

The problems with this line of thought are well-known and I will not dwell on them for long. The main problem can be laid out as follows: surely, it seems far fetched to say that we can confer legitimacy to just any old thing by consent. At least, certain conditions regarding non-coercion, rationality, knowledge about the consequences etc. must be fulfilled. However, not all cultures are equal when it comes to providing these conditions for fair individual choice. It is small wonder that women who have been raised in a misogynist culture come to perpetuate gender inequality by "choice". We should not be surprised if people born into illiberal theocratic cultures turn their backs on liberal values, or even turn against them. In short: even if an agent, in word or action, "acquiesces" in illiberal conditions, we have no more than a very weak *prima facie* reason to believe that our duties are fulfilled by letting things be.

Note that Kukathas is well aware that groups and cultures are not internally just or homogenous: There might be gross injustices internally, between the powerful and the disenfranchised, for instance. But this insight is not translated into the awareness that differences in power might very well imply that some individuals do not freely consent to their culturally defined position, but are rather coerced into it. The right to be left alone presupposes that the culture abides by liberal principles. Liberal principles should take priority over cultural rights.

In sum: where Halbertal and Margalit go too far in positing a strong positive duty on citizens and states of majority culture(s) to sustain illiberal minority cultures, Kukathas does not go far enough in imposing a strong positive duty on citizens and the state to interfere in the affairs of illiberal cultures when failing to do so violates or undermines the basic rights of individuals, whether or not these individuals have consented or not.

Cultural Rights as Distributional Rights

By far the most discussed and influential attempt to ground cultural rights within a liberal framework has been developed by Kymlicka (Kymlicka 1989 and 1995). As briefly presented in the above, Kymlicka's basic idea is to view cultural rights as a question of distributional justice. Following Rawls and Dworkin, our distributional fate should not be decided by factors that are beyond our control. But our culturally given horizons, and among them our culturally embedded preferences, are largely or even wholly arbitrary. Often, minorities are less well off in terms of cultural goods than the majority, through no fault of their own. For instance, normally minorities must spend a relatively larger proportion of their personal resources in order to maintain their cultural resources – analogous to the fact that a disabled person might have to spend a larger proportion of his or her resources in order to buy needed medicine. Hence, compensation is due in order to restore at least rough equality between citizens of a given polity.

But is cultural membership and its corollaries really goods or resources in the way envisaged by liberal egalitarians like Rawls and Dworkin? They are indeed, as the cultural background is part of the "social bases of self-respect" that qualify among the "primary goods" of Rawls' theory, and they can easily be squared with either the basic resources that are up for auction or as a part of the circumstances against which we would wish to take insurance in Dworkin's auction scheme.

Kymlicka's defence of cultural rights avoids many of the problems I have discussed in the above, for he insists that 1) barring some special cases, only cultures that are adequately liberal, i.e., they are governed by and they respect liberal rights and principles, are entitled to the special protection of cultural rights (Kymlicka (1989), pp. 168ff, 195ff) and 2) the rationale of liberal cultural rights is intimately connected with the liberal value of choice and reflectivity, and 3) which means that it is a necessary conditions for the entitlement of cultural rights that the culture in question must provide fair opportunities and the social conditions for autonomy:

> The liberal view I am defending insists that people can stand back and assess moral values and traditional ways of life, and should be given not only the right to do so, but also the social conditions which enhance this capacity (e.g., a liberal education)[22]

and

> [Support for fundamentalist or other illiberal communities] ... undermines the very reason we had for being concerned with cultural membership – that it allows for meaningful individual choice.[23]

So far, so good. The question is whether this really provides as safe and sound an argument for cultural rights as Kymlicka believes it does. I will raise two objections. The first follows Okin's argument in (1998, pp. 678ff) rather closely. This objection raises doubts about the degree to which we best serve individuals' interest by respecting their culturally given preferences or circumstances or not. The second targets some of Kymlicka's luck egalitarian premises and is considerably more controversial: it questions the fact that cultural circumstances are non-chosen and arbitrary in the way necessary for Kymlicka's argument to succeed in its present form.

Serving Individuals' Interests

What does it mean to say that a given culture provides the conditions – opportunities and capacities – necessary for individuals to enable them to stand back and critically evaluate their way of life? Surely, it must mean more than just formally obeying the laws of a liberal state. We must be prepared to look at and evaluate the *practice* of cultures. It is an unquestionable fact that many cultures do not *in practice* treat members fairly, respect equality of the sexes or in any other relevant aspect, or provide a genuine liberal education. Recall the third reason why liberals cannot ignore culture: the traditional liberal myopia, ignoring the private sphere, is unjustified if we care for the well-being of individuals, for injustices can happen in the private as well as in the public sphere, and such injustices are very often culturally embedded. When we offer special rights for cultures, then, we must be sure that granting those rights will not have illiberal consequences for individuals in those cultures. Okin believes that this will mean that far fewer cultures than what Kymlicka believes will pass the "test of liberality", and hence, even though Kymlicka in theory has provided liberalism with a cogent theory of minority rights, this theory offers very few minority cultures any special rights. This is of course an empirical matter, and can only be properly answered by a piece-by-piece analysis of relevant candidate minority cultures. However, I believe Okin is definitely on the right track: we must look at the practice, not just the formal features, of cultures in order to decide whether they qualify for special support.

Culture: Choice or Circumstance?

A very different point of critique arises from questioning one of the central premises of Kymlicka's theory, namely that cultural circumstances are wholly, or predominantly non-chosen.

To reiterate: Kymlicka extends one of Rawls and Dworkin's central intuitions – that our relative distributional fate should not depend on contingent factors beyond our control; inequalities arising from choice are justified, but inequalities with roots in non-chosen circumstances are not – to the question of culture. We do not choose what culture we are born into. If I happen to be born into a minority culture, that culture is part of my non-chosen circumstances. If this puts me in an unfavourable distributional situation, I am entitled to compensation under a scheme of fair equality (see, e.g., Kymlicka (1989), pp. 182ff).

Kymlicka appeals forcefully to a variant of one of Dworkin's imaginative scenarios: two ships, one quite large, one quite small, shipwreck on a deserted island. They go through the Dworkinian auction for resources, complete with the insurance scheme, only then to find out that the new inhabitants are split into two culturally, linguistically etc. distinct groups (one from the large ship, one from the small.) Now, the newcomers from the small ship will find that they will come to live in a cultural environment that is largely dominated by the majority, "… in their work, and … in the courts, schools, legislatures etc." (Kymlicka (1989), p.188).

Now, Kymlicka stresses that it is not the case that the minority *envies* the *resources* of the majority; rather, it is the fact that "the majority members possess and utilize their resources within a certain, i.e., within their own cultural community." (Kymlicka, loc.cit.) The logic of Kymlicka's line of thought is that there is an important distinction between resources as such, and the environment in which resources are spent (i.e., the culture), and that the latter is among the non-chosen circumstances that cannot legitimise inequalities.

But is it really that obvious that culture is part of the non-chosen circumstances in the way needed for Kymlicka? If we look at culture as preferences – as in "I would prefer that I spent my resources in this-or-that cultural environment" – it becomes harder to distinguish preferences for culture from *tastes*. Dworkin, among others, claim that we should not try to equalise wellbeing by giving more resources to someone who has a harder time utilizing his or her resources due to having expensive tastes (Dworkin 1981, p. 228, (1995), p 301). Dworkin might be wrong, of course, but at least it should be admitted that the view that cultural environment *per se* is not something we should count as a preference, but rather as a background for utilising resources, is controversial.

We cannot avoid metaphysics in this discussion: is it possible for the agent to choose between cultures, so that we can view cultural background as preferences (or adequately preference-like, if you want), or should we see the cultural background as thoroughly intertwined with agency, so that it is impossible for the agent to distance him- or herself from it? Only if the latter is true can Kymlicka argue that cultural background is *wholly* non-chosen and not at all like preferences.

Here we must note that Kymlicka elsewhere argues in a way that makes it unclear to which extent cultural background is wholly non-chosen:

> ... we don't think that ... self-discovery replaces or forecloses judgements about how to lead our life. *We don't consider ourselves trapped by our present attachments, incapable of judging the worth of the goals we have inherited* (or ourselves chosen earlier) ... No matter how deeply implicated we find ourselves in a social practice or tradition, we feel capable of questioning whether the practice is a valuable one ...[24]

This line of thought carries much of Kymlicka's brilliant discussion and critique of communitarianism. In his rightly famous defence of Rawls against the communitarian claim that we are "encumbered selves" (and hence, the "ghostly" agent in the original position is a sham), he writes

> What is central to the liberal view is not that we can *perceive* a self prior to its ends, but that we understand our selves to be prior to its ends, *in the sense that no end or goal is exempt from possible re-examination* ... I can always envisage my self without its *present* ends.[25]

But if this is so, it is not clear that I cannot evaluate and revise my present cultural attachments, at least given that certain external factors are met (the conditions for autonomy, in a nutshell.) And if I can do that, it is not clear that we should not view cultural background as on par with preferences rather than as non-chosen circumstances. True, people will then face different challenges: if you are brought up in a linguistically minority culture, you will, *ceteris paribus*, have to spend more resources in the pursuit of many valuable activities. But this should give rise, not to minority or cultural rights, but rather to garden variety compensation under an egalitarian scheme of redistribution.[26]

Kymlickas "no-responsibility" premise (i.e., I am not responsible for my cultural background, and hence, I should be compensated if that background puts me in an unfavourable distributive position) can also be attacked more directly. As mentioned, Kymlicka finds support for his view in the intuition elaborated by Rawls *et al* that our natural and social circumstances are generally not something for which we are responsible etc. But it is far from clear that cultural belonging or membership is isomorphic to bad luck in the lottery of natural and social talents in a way that allows Kymlicka to tap into our intuitions about the (lack of) responsibility and justified compensation as regards inequalities with a root in social and natural circumstances: "Most individuals with handicaps would readily give them up if they could, but they cannot; members of minority cultures are usually not at all willing to give up membership in their culture, but they can." (Danley (1991), p. 176.) Danley distinguishes (rightly, I believe) between circumstances and responses to circumstances: sure, it is plausible that we should not be held responsible for our circumstances, but we *are* responsible – to some extent, at least – for our *responses* to our circumstances.[27] If we had a cheap and reasonably safe cure for deafness, we would not feel an obligation to compensate deaf persons who choose to stay deaf, *even if* they invoked arguments about a special "deaf culture." We might have an obligation to facilitate the transition from one encompassing situation to another (in fact I believe we have at least a *prima facie* duty to do so), but we do not have a duty to respect the choices of persons if these entail unnecessary costs.

Applied to the question of culture and responsibility; it is plausible that we ought not to hold persons responsible for their culture, but it is also plausible that we can hold them responsible – to a certain extent, at least – for their responses to their cultural circumstances. I cannot undertake here to develop a theory of how far this "response responsibility" goes, but it does not seem entirely far fetched to insist that agents are responsible for altering their preferences or their expectations of preference satisfaction in the light of preference-*costs*; hence, insofar it *is* possible for agents to alter their preferences, they have some sort of responsibility for their cultural preferences that make it unreasonable for them to expect that others have a duty to compensate them willy-nilly for their (perhaps expensive) tastes. Exactly how far this responsibility goes is, almost needless to say, an extraordinarily controversial issue.

Several rejoinders to this are possible, but one is especially pertinent. This is the line of thought developed by G.A. Cohen (see Cohen (1999). Cohen argues, famously, that we are *not* necessarily responsible for our tastes, and hence, even though our tastes are expensive, we have a right to be compensated for them if they put us in a negative unequal distributional situation. Or to be more precise: if our tastes are configured (involuntarily, as a matter of constitution, not by our own cultivation) in a way which makes satisfaction of a certain fair (equal, I guess) level of wellbeing *more expensive* than the mean, we are entitled to compensation, in order to equalise our opportunity for welfare.

However, this is only the surface of the argument: In order not to disturb our (I submit) rather robust intuitions concerning responsibility, fair compensation, and expensive tastes, Cohen lumps together a heap of qualifications to the picture that – contrary to his own intents – make it very uncertain whether any person can really claim to be entirely at the mercy of his or her own expensive tastes: First of all, when we say that someone has expensive tastes, we cannot take his or her actual pattern of consumption as an indication of expensive tastes: that "… may show not that her tastes are expensive, but just that her bank balance is large" (Cohen (1999), p. 84). This is plausible. A Hollywood diva fallen on hard times cannot claim that she should be compensated because she has cultivated a preference for fine organic foods and haute couture that cannot be satisfied on a normal salary. Nor can a person who is not willing to settle for less than his or her preferred, expensive choice of consumption, but who is perfectly able to do so, "… [f]or that is a matter not of her tastes as such, but of her stance, of the policy that she adopts when seeking to satisfy her tastes." (Cohen (1999), p. 85).

The kind of expensive tastes that can give grounds for compensation are, as Cohen puts it, a matter of constitution, not behaviour or will. However, at the same time Cohen admits that "… each person's satisfaction function will likely be an amalgam of cheap and expensive tastes, and few may have expensive tastes in an aggregate sense …" (Cohen (1999), p. 85).

I believe this is an important, and basically sound, qualification: for any normal, responsible and reasonable citizen, it is highly unlikely that his or her preferences are uniformly expensive across the board, that there is no way in which he or she can pursue wellbeing that is not relatively close to the mean in terms of cost. This also holds true when we speak of preferences for culture: culture is not one thing, it is made up of a multitude of components and practices, some cheap and some possibly terribly expensive. We should not frustrate persons' preference to speak the language of their choice at home, to worship (within reasonable limits) the deity they want to, or to dance their local dances. But these are rarely costly practices, and if they are, they could normally be changed without losing much of their specific cultural affinity. The point is that, in all but the most extreme of cases, reasonable persons can find cheap or cost-neutral alternatives to their expensive tastes for culture that can satisfy their specific tastes. And if they cannot, they can probably find alternatives to their expensive cultural tastes in other spheres of satisfaction.[28]

In short: the cases in which we have reasonable grounds for believing that a person cannot (as opposed to prefers not to) respond to his expensive tastes in a way which minimises the costs without undermining the possibilities for satisfying a plausible threshold of wellbeing are probably very rare. The exceptionality of such persons makes it highly implausible that it should arise as a *collective* problem, and even more unlikely that it should be a long-lasting collective problem. These rare exceptions should not pose a big challenge for liberal egalitarianism. Especially, we should not count them as being the rule rather than the exception, and hence, they should not occupy a prominent position in our intuitions about liberal justice.

In sum: there are at least two valid points of critique against Kymlicka's defence of cultural rights: first of all, the range of possible candidates for legitimate support might be very small, insofar as we impose the restriction that only sufficiently liberal cultures are legitimate beneficiaries of a scheme of rights etc., and second, that cultural background is not really non-chosen in the way presupposed by Kymlicka's general argument.

Conclusion: Liberal Citizenship

If one wants to argue for a liberal way of dealing with sociological multiculturalism, it might seem that we have reached an impasse. On one hand, as liberals, we cannot allow cultural rights that violate or undermine traditional liberal concerns. On the other, it seems that precisely because of these liberal concerns, we cannot take actions to defend those cultural settings and practices that support liberal values. This seems to imply both that liberalism depends entirely on fortuitous societal and cultural circumstances in which citizens happens to support liberal values,[29] and that liberalism depends on a monocultural setup (or at least one with cultures that are more peaceful and mutually tolerant than what can reasonably be expected) that renders liberalism incompatible with sociological multiculturalism.

However, liberalism need not be in this predicament. If we dispense with the demand of neutrality, we are able to take action in contested areas of civil society, among other things with an eye to the necessary cultural conditions for a liberal society and a liberal state.

In the above, I sketched some plausible conditions for rights and some arguments to the effect that liberal political philosophy and practice ought not to ignore culture. I will now return to these subjects in light of the discussion of multiculturalism.

Political rights in a liberal context – indeed, in any plausible context – are circumscribed by two provisos: the "no grossly burdensome duties" and the "only legitimate interests" proviso. Giving out cultural rights simply because some individuals want them, or simply on the basis of cultures themselves – what I called communitarian multiculturalism – threatens to overstep the boundaries of both provisos. Assigning priority to culture per se and imposing positive duties on citizens to protect them might be extremely burdensome: Both for the tax payer *and* for the individuals in an oppressive illiberal culture enjoying special protection. And, even though liberal politics must take people as they are and view the expressed preferences of citizens as at least *prima facie* legitimate, they are not necessarily so.

Arguing for (minority) cultural rights on the grounds of distributional justice is cogent and might buttress the claims of recognition of certain, fairly liberal minority cultures. However, in the light of the criticisms given in the above, it is not obvious that the rights affiliated with Kymlicka *et al's* programme are *cultural* rights (in any sense that implies "rights to a specific culture"): rather, the extent of these rights might go as far as, and not beyond those, of standard egalitarian rights of equal redistribution.

The argument that some sort of cultural rights are necessary for the survival of a liberal regime itself is sound. However, these are rights to a *liberal* culture, and hence, they are unlikely to satisfy the demands of those who wish to extend cultural rights to illiberal cultures.

The argument that a liberal political regime and liberal political philosophy must give up the traditional liberal myopia concerning the private sphere, and hence, the cultural sphere, seems even less accommodating for those who want to assign cultural rights for illiberal cultures. For the point of annulling the bracketing off of the private sphere is exactly that illiberal injustices can happen in the private sphere and/or be embedded in illiberal cultural practices.

As I argued in the above, liberals ought not to ignore culture. Cultural background largely determines the values and personal principles of persons, and moreover, the prospects of wellbeing. But recognising that culture is important and has wide-reaching implications does not necessarily mean that we must value culture *qua* culture, or on the premises of each and every distinct culture, however conceived. Rather, we can plausibly view culture as a legitimate part of the circumstances that are alterable from a political point of view: if this or that culture, or (more often) this or that *part* of a given culture serves genuine human interests that are compatible with liberal values, we can promote human well-being by promoting that culture or cultural element. Doing so might flout the principle of neutrality. Not doing so might undermine any aspiration toward a liberal political order. I believe dispensing with neutrality is the more appealing price to pay. Furthermore, more liberal neutralists now seem to espouse some sort of limited neutrality, allowing that the state can operate in certain, contested areas of social life without jeopardising legitimacy.

The kind of rights most congenial to a perfectionist liberal programme is, I venture, probably not collective cultural rights. It is more likely a form of individualist rights to *a* culture (i.e., a liberal culture, or any culture that is compatible with liberal values) rather than rights to *my present* culture. This does not mean that members of minority cultures cannot plausibly argue that they need special protection or compensation, e.g., due to their speaking a non-majority language, or many other typical claims of minorities. But recognising their special needs is no more recognising their culture *qua* culture than recognising that a disabled person faces tougher challenges than the rest of us is recognising a special "disability culture."

The kind of liberal multiculturalism following from these considerations should focus on *citizenship*: the cultural values to be protected and promoted are the values of, and conditions for, fair and equal membership of a liberal community. This is pluralism rather than monism, for a decent liberal society allows for a broad range of more specific and substantial cultural expressions and allegiances.

Notes

1. I would like to thank Sune Lægaard, Kasper Lippert-Rasmussen, Janet Radcliff Richards, Thomas Søbirk Petersen, and participants at the 2005 Network for Equality and Plurality Seminar for discussions and invaluable advice on early versions of this paper.
2. Some might protest that this is an unnecessarily broad definition: that one should include only such theories that explicitly deal with the challenges of sociological multiculturalism, for instance. However, if a theory has reasonably clear implications for how to deal with these challenges, I for one see no problems with including them in this category.
3. I am cutting some very sharp corners indeed here, but the gist of the story is as follows: Standard liberal neutralists argue that we cannot rely on conceptions of the good in arguing for the ways in which to use the coercive power of the state. Culture and its evaluation rely on different conceptions of the good; hence, we cannot use arguments about culture as arguments in political decisions. That is not to say that the *effects* of a neutralist regime will be the same for all cultures.
4. Of course, some liberal egalitarians do not accept a distinction between choice and circumstance, or do so only in a very weak sense. Basic-income proponents like van Parijs ("Why Surfers Should be Fed") and his ilk seems to say that life-style is fundamentally not something we as individuals are responsible for: our choice of lifestyle or our preferences for a lifestyle is part of our circumstances, not our choices. This is the extreme face of luck egalitarianism (I am not claiming that this is the only face.) Subtleties aside, luck egalitarians claim that we should equalise differences in welfare (or resources) that arise due to differences in circumstances; that only differences that can plausibly be explained as results of choice are legitimate. But if we are not responsible for our choices of lifestyle or our preferences – they might arise as the result of circumstance, e.g., growing up in a family of slackers or having genes that dispose one towards laziness – it seems that either everything is the result of circumstances, or that "choice" is an epiphenomenon of no real moral impact. Hence, we should equalise every difference, including those stemming from different cultural backgrounds. I for one see this whole line of argument, not as a positive argument in favour of far-reaching egalitarianism, but rather as a *reductio ad absurdum* of the claim that whatever we are not responsible for ought not influence (negatively) on our relative distributional fate.
5. For a position that clearly says that the state should, under normal circumstances, support valuable and necessary institutions in the cultural marketplace, see Hurka (1993), esp. pp. 158-60 Even neutralists such as Rawls admit the limits of neutrality under certain conditions: For example, he notes, in passing, that the "… unavoidable consequences of reasonable requirements for children's education may have to be accepted, often with regret." (Rawls (1993), p. 200. Cf.: Kukathas/Pettit, pp. 140f). Se also Rawls (1993), pp. 199f, cf. Rawls (1988), *passim.*
6. Halbertal/Margalit, p. 491, emphasis added.
7. Halbertal/Margalit, p. 505 emphasis added.
8. This gets much more complicated if we factor in coming generations, but I will leave this aside.
9. I presuppose here that a "reasonably just" distribution of goods is *not* sensitive to cultural differences; otherwise, the question becomes redundant.
10. "Trekkies" are devoted fans of the Tv-series Star Trek. Many of those speak an artificial "extra-terrestrial" language, Klingon. "Deadheads" are fanatical fans of the hippie-rock *cum* fringe-culture outfit Grateful dead and especially their late spiritual leader, Jerry Garcia.
11. Against this, it might be suggested that the relevant groups are such that you are *born* into them, whereas the groups I mention here are groups to which you choose to belong. However, some

are born deadheads, it is at least possible that one is born a gay masochist, and why should the contingent specifics of your time and place of birth have any necessary bearing on your rights?
12. A related line of thought directed against Kymlicka is pursued by Danley (see Danley (1991), pp. 173, 175ff), but I will postpone discussion of that critique for now.
13. *Ceteris paribus*, if I am successful as a philosopher, as a father and husband, as a friend and as a hockey player, all at least partially socially defined pursuits, I have high levels of personal wellbeing.
14. I hasten to add that this article might be a very bad example of this striving for originality ...
15. Here I disregard extreme cases of assimilation of cultures by military conquest etc.
16. Perhaps liberal pessimists tend to overdo the resilience of illiberal cultures; perhaps liberal optimists are too carefree about this. Unfortunately, I have not been able to track down persuasive empirical studies of this.
17. For a related criticism, see Yack, p. 169 *et circa*.
18. Rawls (1993), p. 32. To refresh the reader's memory – though I am sure I do not need to – Rawls is speaking of individuals, not cultures or communities.
19. When we change the individuals of a minority culture into individuals of the majority, there will be a loss of wellbeing, or there will be breaches of rights.
20. Just to kill a possible rejoinder before it muddies the waters: the relevant condition cannot simply be the formal one that the content of the culture is mine: there are no sound reasons to believe that agents cannot change their sense of belonging from one culture to another over time, and hence, freeze framing the picture so that the relevant relations of belonging to cultures is the relations of one moment in time is just conservatism for conservatisms' sake.
21. After several readings of the relevant texts, I am still not too sure about how these limits are conceived.
22. Kymlicka (1995), p. 92, cf.: Okin (1998), p. 678.
23. Kymlicka (1989), pp. 171f, cf.: Okin (1998), p. 678.
24. Kymlicka (1989), pp. 53f, emphasis added.
25. Kymlicka (1989), p. 52, emphasis in original.
26. One might make an indirect defence of cultural rights by saying that, instrumentally, it is a very effective way of achieving fair equality of resources if we grant certain cultures certain rights. However, I am pretty sure that such a suggestion is far more modest than what Kymlicka has in mind.
27. I am well aware that the debate over responsibility extremely controversial and complicated; however, I tend to believe that for as long as we haven't seen any true knock down arguments against the idea of responsibility, we should not be tempted to give up the idea entirely. At the very least, I gather that only extreme advocates of a general "no responsibility"-thesis will deny the instrumental value of holding some persons responsible in some circumstances, and what I sketch in the above is – again, at the very least – one such example.
28. This does not impugn Cohen's contention that "[the fact that most people do not, on aggregate, have expensive tastes] ... is irrelevant to the philosophical question, which is whether or not expensive tastes warrant compensation ..." (Cohen (1999), p.85.) But it limits the case, I believe, to a minimum of persons so small that they are better viewed, not as a class of persons that can make a collective claim of cultural rights, but rather as severely handicapped and unfortunate individuals that merit care and compassion *as individuals*.
29. Of course, optimistic liberals will argue that, once people experience life in a liberal political state, they will more or less automatically come to endorse liberal values. I disagree, not because I believe that liberal values are not strong or good, but because I believe that [competing values, fragility of traditional liberal defences, weakness of the will].

Literature:
Ackerman, Bruce (1980) *Social Justice in the Liberal State* (New Haven; Yale University Press)
Cohen, G.A.(1997) "Where the Action is: On the Site of Distributive Justice", *Philosophy and Public Affairs* Vol. 26 #1
(1999) "Expensive Tastes and Multiculturalism", pp. 80-100 in Bhargava *et al* (eds.) *Multiculturalism, Liberalism and Democracy*, (Oxford: Oxford University Press)
Danley, John (1991) "Liberalism, Aboriginal Rights, and Cultural Minorities", *Philosophy and Public Affairs*, Vol. 20, No. 2, pp. 168-185
Dworkin, Ronald (1981) "What is Equality? Part 1: Equality of Welfare", *Philosophy and Public Affairs*, Vol. 10, #3
(1983) "Neutrality, Equality, and Liberalism", in MacLean and Mills (eds.) *Liberalism Reconsidered* (New Jersey; Rowman and Allanheld)
(1995) "Foundations of Liberal Equality" (*FLE*), in Stephen Darwall (ed.), *Equal Freedom (Selected Tanner Lectures on Human Values)*, (Ann Arbor; The University of Michigan Press)
Edmundson, William A. (1998) *Three Anarchical Fallacies* (Cambridge; Cambridge University Press)
Halbertal, Moshe, and Margalit, Avishai (1994) "Liberalism and the Right to Culture", *Social Research* 61 (491-510)
Kukathas, Chandran (1992) "Are There Any Cultural Rights?", *Political Theory*, Vol. 20, (105-139)
(1998) "Liberalism and Multiculturalism", *Political Theory* Vol. 26, (686-699)
Kymlicka, Will (1989) *Liberalism, Community, and Culture* (Oxford: Clarendon Press)
(1995) *Multicultural Citizenship: A Liberal Theory of Minority Rights* (Oxford: Oxford University Press)
Larmore, Charles E. (1987) *Patterns of Moral Complexity* (Cambridge; Cambridge University Press)
Okin, Susan Moller (1989) *Justice, Gender, and the Family* (New York; Basic Books)
(1998) "Feminism and Multiculturalism: Some Tensions", *Ethics*, Vol. 108, #4 (661-684)
Rawls, John (1971) *A Theory of Justice* (Oxford; Oxford University Press)
(1993) *Political Liberalism* (New York; Colombia University Press)
Raz, Joseph (1986) *The Morality of Freedom* (Oxford; Clarendon)
(1994) "Multiculturalism: A Liberal Perspective", pp. 170-192 in *Ethics in the Public Domain* (rev. ed.) (Oxford; Oxford University Press)
Yack, Bernard: (1988) "Liberalism and its Communitarian Critics: Does Liberal Practice 'Live Down' to Liberal Theory?" in: "*Community in America: the Challenge of Habits of the Heart*", eds. Reynolds, Charles, Norman, Ralph, University of California Press, Berkeley 1988

QUANTUM REALISM: THE INTERPRETATION OF AN INTERPRETATION?

JAN FAYE

Department of Media, Cognition and Communication
University of Copenhagen

Jens Hebor, *The Standard Conception as Genuine Quantum Realism*. Odense: University Press of Southern Denmark 2005, 231 s.

Every physical theory needs an interpretation. Physical theories are meant to represent something different from themselves, and it is characteristic of them that they are expressed in terms of mathematics, which implies that the mathematical symbols must be assigned a physical meaning in order for these theories to be relevant for a physical description of some particular phenomenon. This form of interpretation is the proper physical reading. Another more global form of interpretation is the metaphysical construal of a theory. It attempts to understand what the basic formulas tell us about the world and whether we should be realist or antirealist with respect to the theory and entities in question.

In general a physical interpretation operates by relating the mathematical symbols with already well-known physical terms based on representational conventions. The trained physicist therefore understands the use of the mathematical symbols in the context of a specific theory without being involved in any act of interpretation. This he does to the extent that the representational conventions are part of the physical practise and background knowledge as is the case as long as the theory is used within its standard repertoire of applications. But a new theory may introduce mathematical terms which have no counterparts in old theories. A nice example is the Dirac matrice. It stands for spin in quantum mechanics which is not identical with the classical angular momentum. Here one cannot rely on the classical convention in reaching an understanding of what the symbol stands for or what it means. Physicists must keep on interpreting the meaning until a common understanding of that expression crystallizes. This happens when its representational structure is laid down with respect to the experimental practise and physical data.

The situation is quite different with respect to the metaphysical interpretation of a theory. All metaphysical interpretations are grossly underdetermined by data and will always be. Whereas a physical interpretation eventually becomes established as the shared understanding of a particular physical theory, a metaphysical interpretation is always debatable without further empirical findings.

In philosophy of physics there is an ongoing metaphysical dispute about whether the standard theory of quantum mechanics should be interpreted realistically or non-realistically, and if it should be interpreted realistically, what kind of realist ontology one might coherently extract from the mathematical formalism. The motivation hereof is based on two insights. On the one hand, a literal mathematical interpretation identifies physical reality with a mathematical model of operators. Such a model is the abstract Hilbert space. On the other hand, a literal physical reading takes the physical understanding of the theory at face value. This suggests a physical reality very different from the world of classical physics. It is a reality which consists of value-indefiniteness, superposition, entanglement, intrinsic probabilities, and measurement collapse. In both cases, it leaves us with an understanding of physical reality which is very unfamiliar. Therefore, many philosophers, regardless of their overall attitude to realism and non-realism, do not think of any of them as constituting a satisfactory metaphysical understanding.

In his book *The Standard Conception as Genuine Realism*, the Danish philosopher Jens Hebor takes part in this debate. As the title indicates, Hebor is a proponent of a realist interpretation of quantum mechanics. He urges that the quantum formalism should be interpreted realistically and that the only correct realist interpretation corresponds with what he takes to be the standard interpretation. "By the standard conception of quantum mechanics I refer to the rational core of what is often called the Copenhagen interpretation or the orthodox view." (p.13) The standard conception includes, according to Hebor, value-indefiniteness, superposition, entanglement, non-separability, intrinsic probability, and measurement collapse. Other realist interpretations such as the many-world-interpretation, the Bohmian interpretation, and the modal interpretation are dismissed as absurd or incoherent.

To reach his goal Hebor makes clear that we must distinguish between realism and ontology as well as between realism as such and classical realism. Realism is compatible with many different ontologies, i.e. theories about the nature and structure of the world. Realism is merely the metaphysical view that no matter what is claimed to exist, it exists independently of the human mind or cognitive capacity. Hebor takes it to be a fallacy, which he calls the ontology-realism fallacy, i.e. associating a definite ontology with realism. Thus, he argues that physical realism cannot, and should not, be identified with classical realism. I completely agree. Hebor also argues that even classical realism may cover different ontologies. I concur too.

What then is classical realism? It is a set of requirements which an interpretation of any physical theory has to meet to be called a classical interpretation of that theory. Some of these requirements have their origin in our common sense view of reality which rests on our common practise of identification, discrimination and interaction. According to Hebor, classical realism can be characterized by ten different features or requirements. These are briefly: (1) *Classical state-observable structure* which implies that physical quantities (properties) are measurable in principle. In other words, physical quantities are observables. (2) *Value-definiteness*, i.e. every observable has a definite value at all times. (3) *Space-time dependence*. Classical observables are defined on space and time in the sense that they are a function thereof. (4) *Non-superposition of states*. A physical system always has a definite state so that any observable pertaining to that state is always definite and determinate. (5) *Separability*. In a composite system which consists of spatially separated subsystems each and every subsystem will be in a definite state. (6) *Continuity*. All interactions are continuous in nature such that all those values represented by real numbers exist between the initial and final state of a system. (7) *Classical description*. All observed systems can be described as if they are unobserved, and if not, it is possible to correct for the possible influences due to the observation. (8) *Completeness*. All observables pertaining to a system (at any other time) are determined by the present state of the system. (9) *Objectivity*. A physical description of a physical system is objective in the sense that the description represents the system as it really is. And (10) *Classical realism*. This is the core assumption according to which physical systems exist independently of any description and they are always in a definite state having definite values. Some of these requirements are more epistemological than ontological, none of them are controversial, but I find Hebor's attempt to make a structured explication of these requirements of much value because it paves the way to a constructive discussion of quantum ontology and possible realist interpretations of quantum mechanics.

It is worth mentioning that it is not only classical physical theories, like Newtonian mechanics, thermodynamics, statistical mechanics and Maxwellian electrodynamics, which arguably fit the interpretation of classical realism. Also the special theory of relativity and the general theory of relativity can in general be given such an interpretation, even though there are some problems in connection with the general theory of relativity. But when it comes to quantum mechanics, it is no longer possible to keep a classical understanding.

I think Hebor provides us with a realist interpretation of quantum mechanics which is both original and independent of other realist interpretations of quantum mechanics. What he does, in my opinion, is rather straightforward: he looks at the quantum formalism and sees what it takes to give a realist interpretation of the formalism bearing in mind its physical interpretation. He figures that out by taking the physically interpreted formalism at face value as a possible metaphysical interpretation, and then he regards it as the only genuine realist interpretation of quantum phenomena. Here he has done a pretty good job, I think, since he is perhaps the first philosopher who has taken seriously the full philosophical consequences of such a literal reading. Not only does he argue that quantum systems are real, but so are quantum states with dislocalized position and indeterminate momentum, superposition, entanglement, and quantum collapse. I wonder, however, why he does not discuss in this connection Ghirardi, Rimini, and Weber's (GRW) theory of the collapse of the wave function. This theory is not a part of standard quantum mechanics although it seems to contain some of the features Hebor attributes to the orthodox theory.

In addition – and indeed in most beautiful support of his own account – Hebor rejects other acclaimed realist interpretations for being incoherent. Much of this criticism reflects beliefs with which other philosophers can associate themselves. Hebor takes issue with the many-world interpretation, the decoherence view, the modal view, and the Bohmian theory. Some of the criticism is well-taken; especially with regards to the many world interpretation and the Bohmian theory, other parts are perhaps less convincing such as his criticism of the modal and the decoherence view. I shall leave the more technical issues aside. I will only make one substantial remark concerning Hebors' handling of these other realist approaches, namely that he states his own reservations too presumptuously as if there exists a proof of his own view and a disproof of those he disagrees with. Nobody in the world can prove or disprove a metaphysical interpretation. In general, metaphysics is a shaky business.

In my opinion Hebor has given a very coherent interpretation of quantum mechanics in which he takes many aspects into considerably technical consideration. Apart from technical details, I think, nonetheless, that his over-all view can be called into question in two ways. First, what are the philosophical arguments for being a full-blown realist about scientific theories, and say, not only a realist about entities? Second, is it correct that the standard conception of quantum mechanics, as Hebor understands it, was seen by Bohr as a realist interpretation?

Many philosophers believe that physical theories are empirically underdetermined by data. In my opinion this also holds in the domain of the quantum world. There are revival theories to the orthodox quantum mechanics which does not merely signal another interpretation of the standard theory like the many world interpretation or the modal interpretation. Bohm's theory of a quantum potential is such an alternative theory which gives the same kind of predictions as the orthodox quantum theory. Both theories assume the existence of atomic particles, but interpreted realistically they attribute to the system very different properties. Thus, Hebor's argument still needs some very strong arguments showing that one should be realist concerning the orthodox theory of quantum mechanics, arguments which he does not present to us in the present book. Rather, regarding Bohr's view as an example of entity realism, as does Henry Folse, seems a much more compelling view because this makes neither quantum mechanics nor Bohm's theory literally true.

Realism occurs with different commitments. It may come in degrees and contain other than an ontological component. One may be a realist about ontology but not with respect to semantics or epistemology. Such a realist would not hold the same form of realism as one who is a realist with respect to ontology, semantics and epistemology. But Hebor's view of realism is not particularly complex. According to him, realism merely maintains the existence of a mind-independent world whose properties are what they are independently of our cognitive capacity. From his realist interpretation of the standard quantum theory it is evident that he takes a realistic approach to semantics and epistemology as well.

The title of the book clearly shows that Hebor believes that it is not only the orthodox theory of quantum mechanics which can be given a wholly realist understanding. He also holds that the *standard conception is a realist interpretation of the quantum world*, assuming furthermore that the rational core of the Copenhagen interpretation is the only coherent realist understanding. In all fairness he admits that physicists like Bohr, Heisenberg, Pauli and Born – who each saw himself as a spokesperson for the spirit of Copenhagen – have given different explanations of what that implied. Bohr is nevertheless the person whom everybody regards as the "spiritual" leader. When it comes to a close reading of Bohr's work, Hebor is not sufficiently attentive to detail. It would require a closer scrutiny to persuasively defend a view that differs from most other realist as well as antirealist readings of Bohr.

On p. 51 he says: "Now, without going too much into the issue here it may be emphasized that Bohr definitely was a realist about quantum systems ... and about Planck's constant." Every contemporary philosopher who has studied Bohr's work is likely to accept this. Hebor then continues: "Bohr didn't say very much about states and observables and what he said was typically in the form of a warning against pictorial readings of the state vector." This is correct too. But he adds: "I do think, however, that Bohr actually was a realist about these items ... too – even though Bohr of course was not a classical realist concerning the relation between states and observables ... I think that Bohr ought to be a realist concerning these items, too, if his understanding of quantum mechanics is to be at all coherent." But what if Bohr were an entity realist and a theory antirealist, then would he be incoherent?

Some philosophers, including myself, see Bohr as a realist about system but an antirealist about states without being incoherent. But I think that everybody must admit that Bohr is notoriously opaque in his writings and that some of his wordings may be interpreted one way or the other. It is impossible to give a satisfactory documentation of my own understanding at this place, but let me make a couple of comments on another of Hebor's passages concerning Bohr and quantum states. On p. 55 he develops his claim a bit further:

> Later Bohr referred to the state vector as "giving the symbolic representation of [the system's] state" ... which of course means that (1) the system *has a state*, (2) the state is *represented by the state vector*, but (3) the representation is *symbolic*, that is, it is not visualizable. It should also be clear that, when Bohr uses the word "symbolic", it definitely does not mean e.g. "purely mathematical" (in that case *symbolic representation* would be a *contradictio in adjecto*) and hence does not commit Bohr to some kind of anti-realism about states.

Naturally enough, a representation must represent something different from itself. The way Hebor sees it is that the state vector gets its physical significance and reality in conjecture with operators; i.e., symbols for *possible* observations.

So the question is what Bohr meant by calling the state vector or the wave function a *symbolic* representation. Usually symbolic language stands in contrast to literal language. Bohr associated the latter form of representation with what can be visualized in space and time. Quantum systems are not visualizable because they cannot be tracked down in space and time as classical systems. The reason is according to Bohr that the mathematical formulation of quantum states consists of imaginary numbers. Thus, the state vector is symbolic. But what if "symbolic" means that the state vector's representational function should not be taken literally but be considered as a *tool* of calculation of probabilities of observables? Let me present one quotation of Bohr's in which he directly says what I just have indicated:

> The entire formalism is to be considered as a tool for deriving predictions of definite or statistical character, as regards information obtainable under experimental conditions described in classical terms and specified by means of parameters entering into the algebraic or differential equations of which the matrices or the wave-functions, respectively, are solutions. These symbols themselves, as is indicated already by the use of imaginary numbers, are not susceptible to pictorial interpretation; and even derived real functions like densities and currents are only to be regarded as expressing the probabilities for the occurrence of individual events observable under well defined experimental conditions. (Bohr 1948[1998]: 144)

Also consider the following: (a) in many places Bohr talks about the mathematical formalism of quantum mechanics as the mathematical *symbolism*, and he talks about *symbolic operators*; (b) concerning the aim of science Bohr says: "In our description of nature the purpose is not to disclose the real essence of phenomena, but only to track down as far as possible relations between the manifold aspects of our experience" (Bohr 1929[1985]: 18); (c) "within the frame of the quantum mechanical formalism, according to which no well defined use of the concept of "state" can be made as referring to the object separate from the body with which it has been in contact, until *the external conditions involved in the definition of this concept* are unambiguously fixed by a further suitable control of the auxiliary body" (Bohr 1938b[1998]: 102, my emphasis) – in other words, it makes no sense to say that a quantum system has a definite kinematical or dynamical state prior to any measurement. Hence we can only ascribe a certain state to a system given those circumstances where we epistemically have access to their realization. Based on these and other considerations, I still think it makes good sense to argue that Bohr was a realist with respect to atomic systems but antirealist with respect to their states.

As a consequence of his realist position on the state vector, Hebor believes that the state of superposition collapses when a measurement is performed on the system. Says he: "As the states are real, the change of state is real too, so collapse is a real physical process." (p.66) But if it is correct, as I have argued, that Bohr was not a realist concerning quantum states, it follows that Bohr didn't believe that the measurement of a quantum system creates a collapse of the wave function. Sure, had he embraced state vector realism and operator realism, he should also by necessity have the collapse of the wave function. But he never did that. In fact, I don't know of any place where Bohr talks about the collapse of the wave function. Hebor's attitude is very Popperian at this point since he seems to regard probabilities as a kind of objective propensities. If Bohr thought that the state vector-cum-operator formalism represented the real *physical* (in contrast to logical) possibilities of observation and that a measurement reduces one of these objective possibilities to actuality when it results in an eigenvalue of the measured observable, why did he not say that explicitly? Rather Bohr had the opinion that the state vector-cum-operator represented the *logical* conditions under which it made sense to ascribe a kinematic or a dynamic property to the system. The actual measurement then gives us the *physical* condition under which we correctly can ascribe a particular such property. It was because of this reason and this alone that he called the state vector and the operators symbolic.

Besides our major disagreement, I also have some minor, but formal, complaints about the book. I find it rather tedious to read a small book containing 230 pages of which 60 pages are notes. It is too demanding of a reader to stop his reading every minute or so. An author does not have to tell the world everything he has read and doesn't like. In my opinion it should be more or less a golden rule that what cannot be incorporated into the main text should be left out. I also wonder why Hebor hasn't acknowledged the person who acted as the linguistic editor of his English text in the Preface. Finally an Index would have helped that reader who wants to study the book more closely.

In his attempt to give a realist interpretation of the orthodox quantum mechanics Hebor has written an impressive book which deserved an international readership. Even though he is self-taught in both physics and mathematics, he masters the mathematical foundation of the discussion apart from showing great philosophical common sense. Whatever our differences on Bohr and quantum mechanics might be, I think that his book demonstrates an innovative insight in quantum mechanics and its possible philosophical implications.

Literature:

Bohr, Niels (1985) *Atomic Theory and the Description of Nature*. The Philosophical Writings of Niels Bohr. Vol. 1. Woodbridge, Conn.: Ox Bow Press.

Bohr, Niels (1998): *Causality and Complementarity. The Philosophical Writings of Niels Bohr*. Vol. 4. (eds. Jan Faye & Henry Folse) Woodbridge, Conn.: Ox Bow Press.

TOWARDS AN INTEGRATION OF MAINSTREAM AND FORMAL EPISTEMOLOGY

PETER ØHRSTRØM

Department of Communication and Psychology
Aalborg University

In his new book, 'Mainstream and Formal Epistemology' [2006], Vincent F. Hendricks (VFH) focuses on the two important traditions in modern epistemology:
- Mainstream epistemology including 'traditional' approaches such as epistemic reliabilism, counterfactual epistemology, and contextual epistemology.
- Formal approaches to epistemology including logical epistemology, computational epistemology, and modal operator epistemology.

Within mainstream epistemology, the aim is to find necessary and sufficient conditions for obtaining and possessing knowledge. The search for such conditions has often made relied on common-sense reasoning based on various examples and counterexamples. In the first part of the book, VFH offers a nice and readable presentation of this tradition, according to which a human agent Ξ knows a proposition h if and only if

1. Ξ believes h
2. h is true
3. Ξ is justified in believing h.
(p.13)

This classic tripartite definition of knowledge has given rise to a number of problems and questions. However, it appears that the third condition is the most problematic. The notion of justification certainly deserves a further (and also very careful) analysis. As a whole, the above definition has been seriously challenged by the socalled Gettier paradoxes going back to Edmund Gettier's highly influential article in 1963, "Is knowledge justified true belief?" [1963]. VFH's new book contains a well written presentation of the Gettier paradoxes (p. 20 ff.) as well as mainstream discussions of them in terms of Alvin Goldman's reliabilism (p. 40 ff.) and Robert Nozick's counterfactual epistemology (p. 52 ff.).

VFH uses formal logic in his discussion of mainstream epistemology, in particular when dealing with counterfactual epistemology (chapter 4) and contextual epistemology (chapter 5). However, in the second part of the book, VFH demonstrates even more clearly the usefulness of philosophical logic within the discussion of fundamental epistemological problems. The formal approaches to epistemology using traditional modal logic and possible worlds semantics are carefully discussed in (chapter 6). This is done in terms of knowledge operators like K_Ξ, where $K_\Xi A$ stands for the proposition that the agent Ξ knows that A, where A is some proposition. Using this formalism it becomes possible to formally discuss which of the various systems of modal logic (S4, S4.2, S4.3, S4.4, S5) will be the best representation of the logic of knowledge we are actually using in our philosophical and everyday discussions. VFH's analysis also makes it possible to enrich the discussion of the problems regarding the perspectives of inquiry taking into account the notions of first-person versus third person. In addition, using this formalism, VFH shows how the discussion can be expanded to a multi-agent setup which supports the view that agents in cooperation will often have to take into account what the other agents in question know at a certain time (p. 105 ff.).

In chapter 7, VFH deals with computational epistemology, which, strictly speaking, is not about knowledge, but rather about knowledge acquisition (or learning). This chapter is written in the context of the investigations carried out by Kevin T. Kelly [1996, 1998a, 1998b]. VFH accepts Kelly's approach according to which a learning strategy solves a learning problem just in case it is admitted as a potential solution by the problem and succeeds in the specified sense over the relevant possibilities (p. 115). In other words, the basic idea is to find methods that succeed in every possible world within a given range. This means that, in computational epistemology, learning is not seen as an independent process but rather as a procedure closely related to a learning method.

VFH illustrates the procedure of computational epistemology with reference to the classical discussion about statements such as "all ravens are black". He considers a Popperian bold method, Ξ, according to which it is conjectured that all ravens are black, as soon as the first black raven is observed. He also considers the skeptical method, θ, which is much more cautious, and which may be understood as an attempt to proceed in an infallible way not accepting anything beyond what the evidence entails. It is obvious that the two methods, Ξ and θ, will produce very different outputs in their attempts to obtain knowledge. In fact, it should be noted that even if all ravens are actually black, then the method $-\theta$ will never come up with this result, whereas the method Ξ will although it will never be able to unambiguously signal when it obtained the correct answer. VFH makes it very clear that in order to reliably solve the epistemic problem, the limit is needed (p. 118). The temporal aspects turns out to be very important, because if a method solves an epistemic problem, the method will generally do so by converging to a correct output. VFH points out that "solvability is in general acutely sensitive to the temporal arrangement of the evidence" (p. 126).

VFH does not present the logical or mathematical details involved in computational epistemology. For such purposes, he mainly refers to the works of Kevin T. Kelly, with whom VFH and O. Schulte published an interesting paper on "Reliable Belief Revision" [1996]. In his new book, however, VFH's emphasis is on the conceptual notions underlying the idea of computational epistemology. The example used by VFH is very simple, but does in fact clearly illustrate that computational epistemology qualifies as an interesting third possibility between pessimistic skepticism and optimistic epistemology.

VFH's discussions of mainstream epistemology and his investigations into traditional logical epistemology and computational epistemology highlight a need for a further development of modal operator epistemology within the context of a temporal logic. The elaboration of this approach is no doubt the most original and interesting contribution in the book (chapter 8). In this chapter, VFH has shown how mainstream theories of knowledge and formal epistemology can be brought together using the ideas of 'forcing' in the context of a temporal logic. In fact, according to VFH, it turns out that mainstream theories of knowledge and formal epistemology have a lot in common. In particular, he points out that the idea of so-called 'forcing' is of common concern. According to VFH, this idea should be viewed as essential for the understanding of epistemology. But what is 'forcing'?

In his former book, *The Convergence of Scientific Knowledge*[2001], VFH has defined 'forcing epistemology' as a family of proposals to answer the skeptic. These proposals are committed to the idea that the way to answer the skeptic, who questions the very possibility of having knowledge, is to agree that real possibilities of error indeed undercut knowledge but that the skeptical possibilities can somehow be ruled out as irrelevant. In his analysis of computational epistemology, VFH has argued that using the idea of "forcing" may in fact enable the transformation of inductive inquiry into "near deductive inquiry." (p. 120) Since knowledge is acquired over time, it is indeed quite obvious that a satisfactory logic of knowledge should be based on a temporal logic. In a process of learning or obtaining knowledge in general, it turns out that the passage of time (and the corresponding loss of relevant future branches in a branching time framework) can be explained in terms of VFH's notion of 'forcing'.

VFH has developed a unified framework in which temporal logic, computation and learning theory are used to articulate and formulate these proposals rigorously. This work has been written in the grand old tradition of trying to combat skepticism and to assure us that human beings can in fact possess knowledge. However, the consequent use temporal logic and branching time is rather new and original. However, there are several kinds of branching time systems.

VFH uses the Priorean idea of branching time (see Øhrstrøm & Hasle 2005), according to which the present moment is conceived as being equivalent with the set of all propositions being true now (including all true statements regarding the past). VFH also chooses to make use of Ockhamistic semantics (p.134 ff.). He represents the possible worlds (futures) in terms of so-called evidence streams (ω-sequences of natural numbers). Following some interesting ideas proposed by K. Kelly [1996], Hendricks has studied a model in which possible worlds are represented as pairs on the form (ε,n), where n is a natural number, and where $\varepsilon = (a_0, a_1, \ldots a_n, \ldots)$ is a so-called evidence stream (i.e. an ω-sequence of natural numbers). The model also includes socalled 'handles' and 'fans':

$\varepsilon = (a_0, a_1, \ldots a_n, \ldots)$	(evidence stream)
(ε,n)	(possible world)
$\varepsilon\|n = a_0, a_1, \ldots a_{n-1}$	(handle)
$[\varepsilon\|n] = \{(\tau,k)\|k\in\omega \text{ and } \tau\|n = \varepsilon\|n\}$	(fan)

Given this formalism, we may speak of the set, M, of all triples on the form (ε,n,a_n). Obviously, all truths about the model follow from the information included in M. On top of the model, VFH has introduced a formal language that includes epistemic modalities. The key notion is a discovery method, δ, i.e. a function that takes a handle $\tau\|n$ as input and produces a hypothesis conceived as a set of possible worlds as output. In fact $\delta(\tau\|n)$ can be read as "the hypothesis (i.e. the suggested knowledge) obtained by the method δ on the basis of

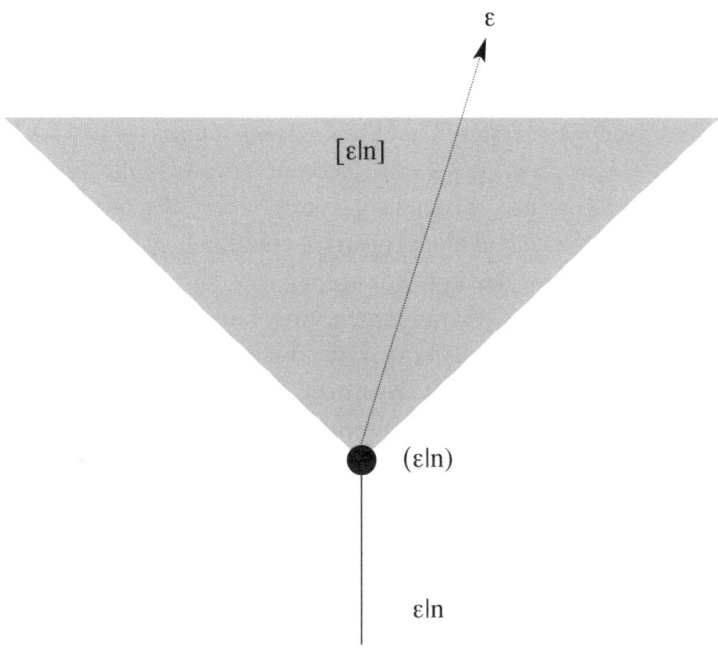

the evidence τ|n". VFH has defined knowledge as limiting convergence, suggesting that δ knows h at (ε,n), if *h* corresponds with M, and if the hypothesis produced by δ will remain unchanged as h after a certain time. Thus, a person using this discovery method may thereby obtain knowledge. In short, the method *knows* something! On the basis of this definition, VFH introduces an epistemic operator, $K_δ$, corresponding to the discovery method, δ. Whether a contingent hypothesis h can be known by a method δ can know anything, will obviously depend on the properties of δ, but it is not ruled out in principle. It might be the case that δ at (ε,n) knows that h is the case at (ε,n'), where n'≥n, although there is some (τ,n') in [ε|n] so that (τ,n') does not belong to *h*. – This possibility clearly illustrates the need for an Ockhamistic tempo-modal logic, as opposed to a Peircean logic which does not accept the idea of truth regarding the contingent future.

VFH limits the discussion in the book to absolute time-invariant empirical hypotheses, h. In fact, he gives a very narrow definition of truth (p. 136). This is a bit surprising, since there can be no doubt that all the results in the book could have been presented in the context of a more traditional temporal logic based on the usual idea of truth.

Defining knowledge as limiting convergence, VFH investigates the logical strength of the resulting modal operator epistemology. Given the semantics sketched here, it is possible to establish a logical tense-logical system extended with the epistemic operator, K_δ. In this system, it turns out that for instance the implication $K_\delta h \supset GK_\delta h$ is a valid theorem. Theorems like this one, which involve temporal as well as epistemic operators, nicely illustrate the interesting formal features of the kind of modal operator epistemology suggested by VFH.

VFH's framework for dealing with agency and epistemic logic in the context of a temporal logic is certainly interesting, but definitely not the only attempt of the kind. As indicated above, crucial aspects of the discussion may be traced back to the works of A.N. Prior (see Øhrstrøm & Hasle 2005). However, a proper theory of agency has to incorporate several other aspects than knowledge. It also has to deal with notions such a belief, desire and obligation. In particular, much attention has been given to the challenge of incorporating deontic logic in a satisfactory manner.

Having established his formalism, it becomes possible for VFH to ask rather precise questions regarding the properties for the K_δ-fragment of the logic. In particular, he studies which conditions K_δ would validate the axioms of the modal logic S4. The crucial axiom is the Axiom 4: $K_\delta h \supset K_\delta K_\delta h$. He argues that this holds if the method δ has the property which he calls 'consistent expectations' (p. 139). From a formal point of view, VFH's result is established convincingly. It is however not made intuitively clear in the book why and how the notion of a 'consistently expectant method' could be conceptually relevant in the context of epistemology.

In the last chapter of the book, chapter 9, VFH comments on some general aspects of modern epistemology. Among other things, he comments on the use of counterexamples in epistemological analysis. It is generally assumed that when discussing a general thesis in epistemology (or other parts of philosophy), the construction of a counterexample can give rise to a very strong argument against the thesis in question. VFH argues, however, that only counterexamples within the range of relevant worlds should be accepted as generators of such crucial arguments. In some cases, such counterexamples turn out to be very speculative and 'way-off thought experiments'. For instance, one may imagine a strange setup somewhere near Alpha Centauri involving infinitely deceiving demons. Some of these examples cannot occur within the range of relevant worlds. Obviously, the problem here is how to distinguish between relevant and non-relevant worlds. In chapter 8, VFH has given some hints referring to 'forcing in time' and 'forcing in worlds' (p. 140), but he does not offer a very precise relevance criterion. It should be admitted that it is possible that nobody can ever provide such a criterion, at least if it has to be formulated in a very precise manner.

In conclusion, it should be emphasized that although 'Mainstream and Formal Epistemology' leaves many interesting questions unanswered, it is definitely a major contribution to epistemology. The unifying concept of "forcing" emphasizes a fruitful and deep investigation of the fundamental questions, which arise on the borderline between logic, epistemology and computation theory. It is VFH's ambition "to merge not only themes from mainstream and formal approaches to epistemology but likewise to bring together tools from different formal epistemologies to accommodate more and more mainstream as well as formal concerns ranging from justification and rationality issues to multi-modal systems and learning" (p. 150). In his book, VFH has presented an elaborated outline of a program towards this ambition. In this way, 'Mainstream and Formal Epistemology' outlines a research program, which is likely to guide future investigations into epistemology, logic and cognitive sciences.

References:
Gettier, E. (1963). "Is knowledge justified true belief?" [1963]. Analysis 23 (6): 121-3.
Kelly, Kevin T., Schulte, O., Hendricks, Vincent F. (1996), "Reliable Belief Revision". In M.L.D Chiara (ed.), *Logic, Methodology, and Philosophy of Science X*. Dordrecht: Kluwer Academic, p. 159-77.
Kelly, Kevin T. (1996). *The Logic of Reliable Inquiry*, New York: Oxford University Press.
Kelly, Kevin T. (1998a). 'Learning Theory and Epistemology'. In M. Sintonen and I. Niniluoto (eds.), Handbook of Epistemology. Dordrecht: Kluwer Academic.
Kelly, Kevin T. (1998b). 'Iterated Belief Revision, Reliability and Inductive Amnesia'. *Erkenntnis* 35: 11-58.
Hendricks, Vincent F. (2006), *Mainstream and Formal Epistemology*, Cambridge University Press 2006.
Hendricks, Vincent F. (2001), *The Convergence of Scientific Knowledge*: A View from the Limit, Kluwer Academic Publishers.
Øhrstrøm, P. & Hasle, P. (2005), 'A.N. Prior's Logic'. In Gabbay, Dov. J.; Woods, John (editors): *Logic and the Modalities in the Twentieth Century. The Handbook of the History of Logic.* Vol. 6, Chapter 5, pp. 323-71. Elsevier.